WYNONNA EARP

BAD DAY AT BLACK ROCK

Become our fan on Facebook facebook.com/idwpublishing
Follow us on Twitter @idwpublishing
Subscribe to us on YouTube youtube.com/idwpublishing
See what's new on Tumblr tumblr.idwpublishing.com
Check us out on Instagram instagram.com/idwpublishing

IDW

Chris Ryall, President and Publisher/CCO
John Barber, Editor-In-Chief
Cara Morrison, Chief Financial Officer
Matt Ruzicka, Chief Accounting Officer
David Hedgecock, Associate Publisher
Jerry Bennington, VP of New Product Development
Lorelei Bunjes, VP of Digital Services
Justin Eisinger, Editorial Director, Graphic Novels & Collections
Eric Moss, Senior Director, Licensing and Business Development

Ted Adams and Robbie Robbins, Founders of IDW

ISBN: 978-1-68405-592-0   22 21 20 19   1 2 3 4

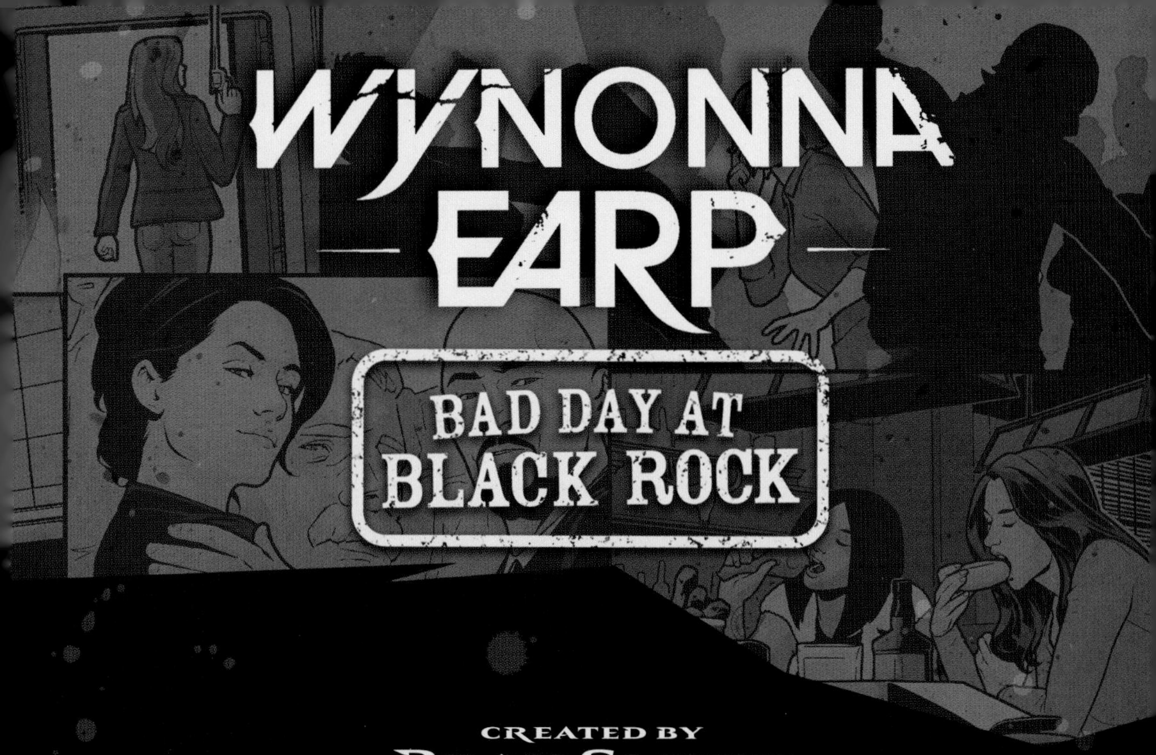

WYNONNA EARP

BAD DAY AT BLACK ROCK

CREATED BY
BEAU SMITH

WRITTEN BY
BEAU SMITH AND TIM ROZON

ART BY
CHRIS EVENHUIS

COLORS BY
JAY FOTOS

COVER ART BY
CHRIS EVENHUIS

LETTERS AND DESIGN BY
CHRISTA MIESNER

EDITOR
DAVID MARIOTTE

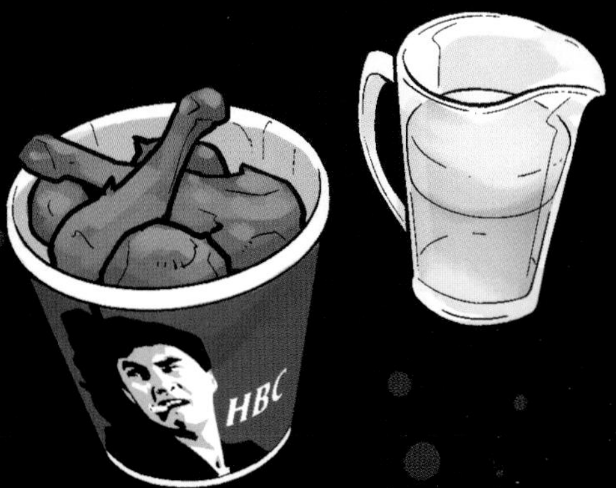
HBC

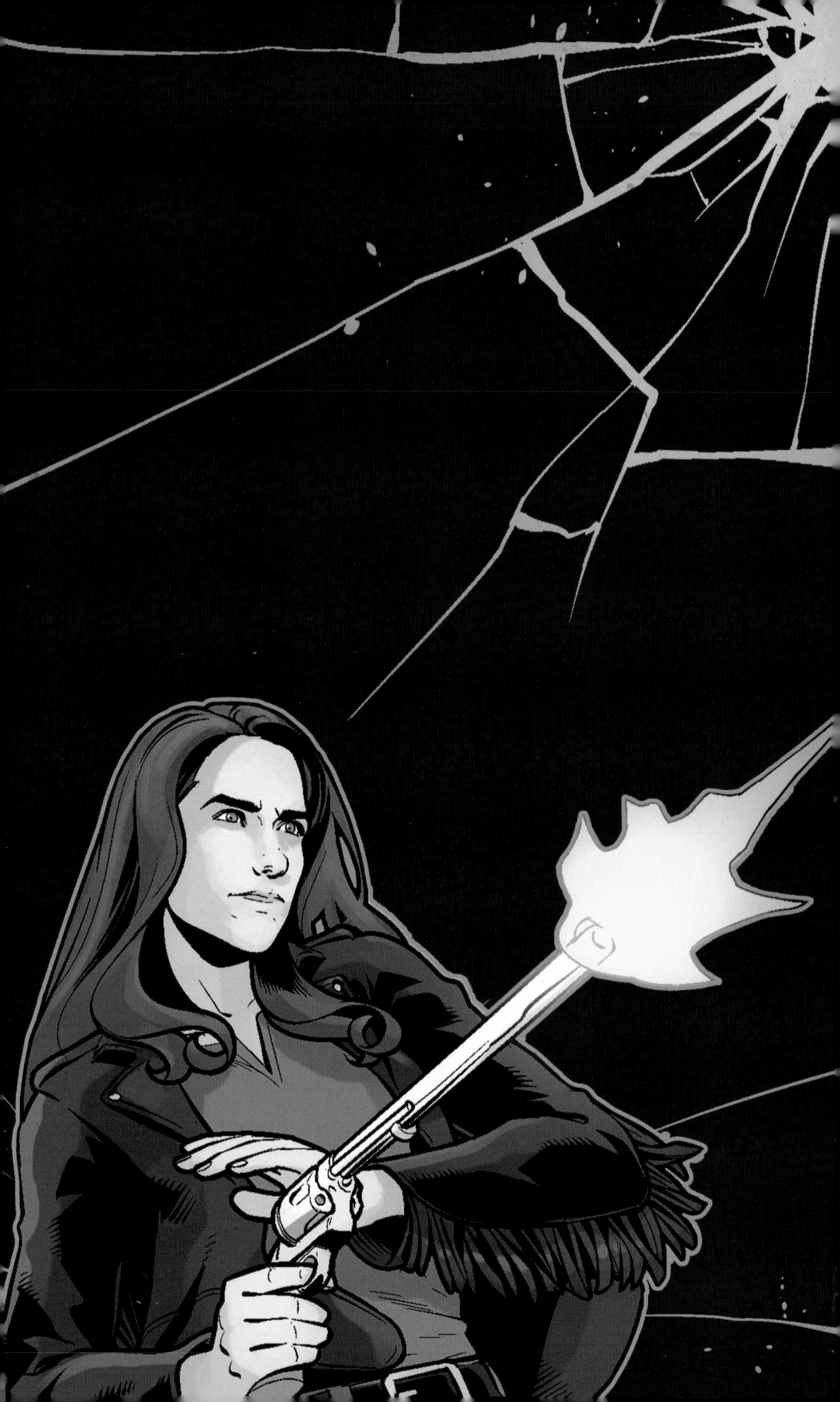

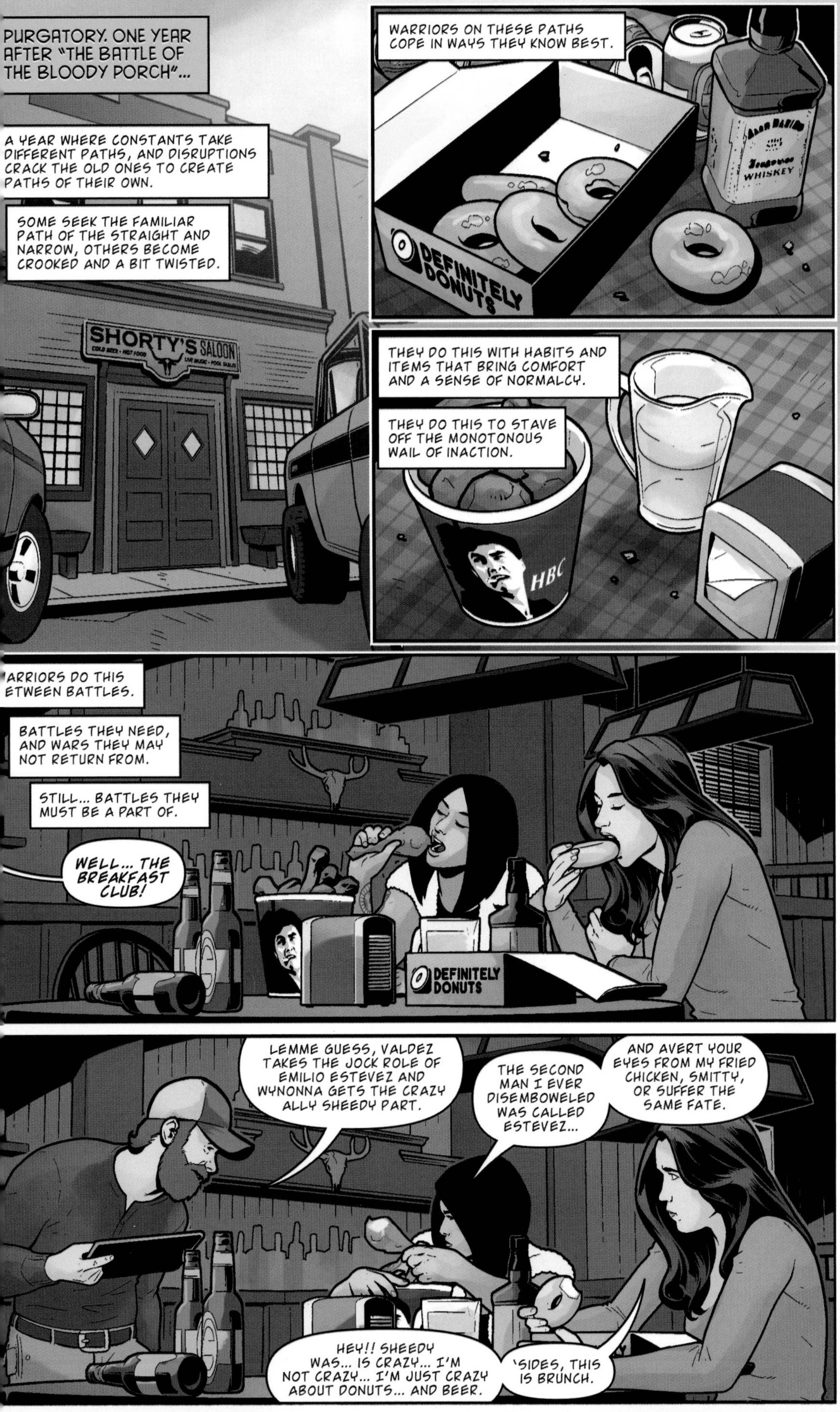

PURGATORY. ONE YEAR AFTER "THE BATTLE OF THE BLOODY PORCH"...
A YEAR WHERE CONSTANTS TAKE DIFFERENT PATHS, AND DISRUPTIONS CRACK THE OLD ONES TO CREATE PATHS OF THEIR OWN.
SOME SEEK THE FAMILIAR PATH OF THE STRAIGHT AND NARROW, OTHERS BECOME CROOKED AND A BIT TWISTED.
SHORTY'S SALOON
COLD BEER · HOT FOOD
LIVE MUSIC · POOL TABLES
WARRIORS ON THESE PATHS COPE IN WAYS THEY KNOW BEST.
DEFINITELY DONUTS
WHISKEY
THEY DO THIS WITH HABITS AND ITEMS THAT BRING COMFORT AND A SENSE OF NORMALCY.
THEY DO THIS TO STAVE OFF THE MONOTONOUS WAIL OF INACTION.
HBC
'ARRIORS DO THIS ETWEEN BATTLES.
BATTLES THEY NEED, AND WARS THEY MAY NOT RETURN FROM.
STILL... BATTLES THEY MUST BE A PART OF.
WELL... THE BREAKFAST CLUB!
DEFINITELY DONUTS
LEMME GUESS, VALDEZ TAKES THE JOCK ROLE OF EMILIO ESTEVEZ AND WYNONNA GETS THE CRAZY ALLY SHEEDY PART.
THE SECOND MAN I EVER DISEMBOWELED WAS CALLED ESTEVEZ...
AND AVERT YOUR EYES FROM MY FRIED CHICKEN, SMITTY, OR SUFFER THE SAME FATE.
HEY!! SHEEDY WAS... IS CRAZY... I'M NOT CRAZY... I'M JUST CRAZY ABOUT DONUTS... AND BEER.
'SIDES, THIS IS BRUNCH.

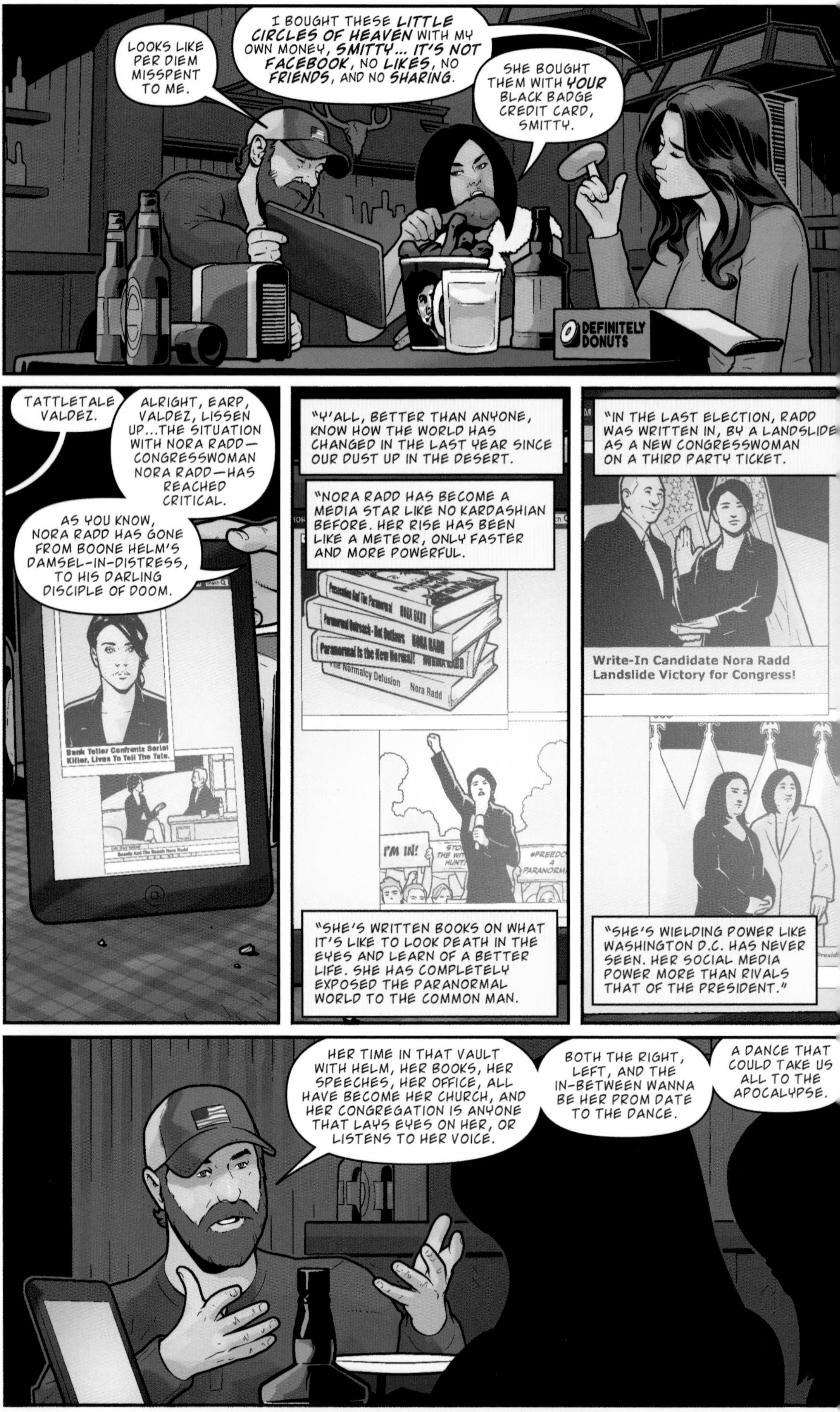
LOOKS LIKE PER DIEM MISSPENT TO ME.
I BOUGHT THESE LITTLE CIRCLES OF HEAVEN WITH MY OWN MONEY, SMITTY... IT'S NOT FACEBOOK, NO LIKES, NO FRIENDS, AND NO SHARING.
SHE BOUGHT THEM WITH YOUR BLACK BADGE CREDIT CARD, SMITTY.
DEFINITELY DONUTS
TATTLETALE VALDEZ.
ALRIGHT, EARP, VALDEZ, LISSEN UP...THE SITUATION WITH NORA RADD—CONGRESSWOMAN NORA RADD—HAS REACHED CRITICAL.
AS YOU KNOW, NORA RADD HAS GONE FROM BOONE HELM'S DAMSEL-IN-DISTRESS, TO HIS DARLING DISCIPLE OF DOOM.
Bank Teller Confronts Serial Killer, Lives To Tell The Tale.
"Y'ALL, BETTER THAN ANYONE, KNOW HOW THE WORLD HAS CHANGED IN THE LAST YEAR SINCE OUR DUST UP IN THE DESERT.
"NORA RADD HAS BECOME A MEDIA STAR LIKE NO KARDASHIAN BEFORE. HER RISE HAS BEEN LIKE A METEOR, ONLY FASTER AND MORE POWERFUL.
Paranormal is the New Normal!
The Normalcy Delusion Nora Radd
I'M IN!
"SHE'S WRITTEN BOOKS ON WHAT IT'S LIKE TO LOOK DEATH IN THE EYES AND LEARN OF A BETTER LIFE. SHE HAS COMPLETELY EXPOSED THE PARANORMAL WORLD TO THE COMMON MAN.
"IN THE LAST ELECTION, RADD WAS WRITTEN IN, BY A LANDSLIDE AS A NEW CONGRESSWOMAN ON A THIRD PARTY TICKET.
Write-In Candidate Nora Radd Landslide Victory for Congress!
"SHE'S WIELDING POWER LIKE WASHINGTON D.C. HAS NEVER SEEN. HER SOCIAL MEDIA POWER MORE THAN RIVALS THAT OF THE PRESIDENT."
HER TIME IN THAT VAULT WITH HELM, HER BOOKS, HER SPEECHES, HER OFFICE, ALL HAVE BECOME HER CHURCH, AND HER CONGREGATION IS ANYONE THAT LAYS EYES ON HER, OR LISTENS TO HER VOICE.
BOTH THE RIGHT, LEFT, AND THE IN-BETWEEN WANNA BE HER PROM DATE TO THE DANCE.
A DANCE THAT COULD TAKE US ALL TO THE APOCALYPSE.

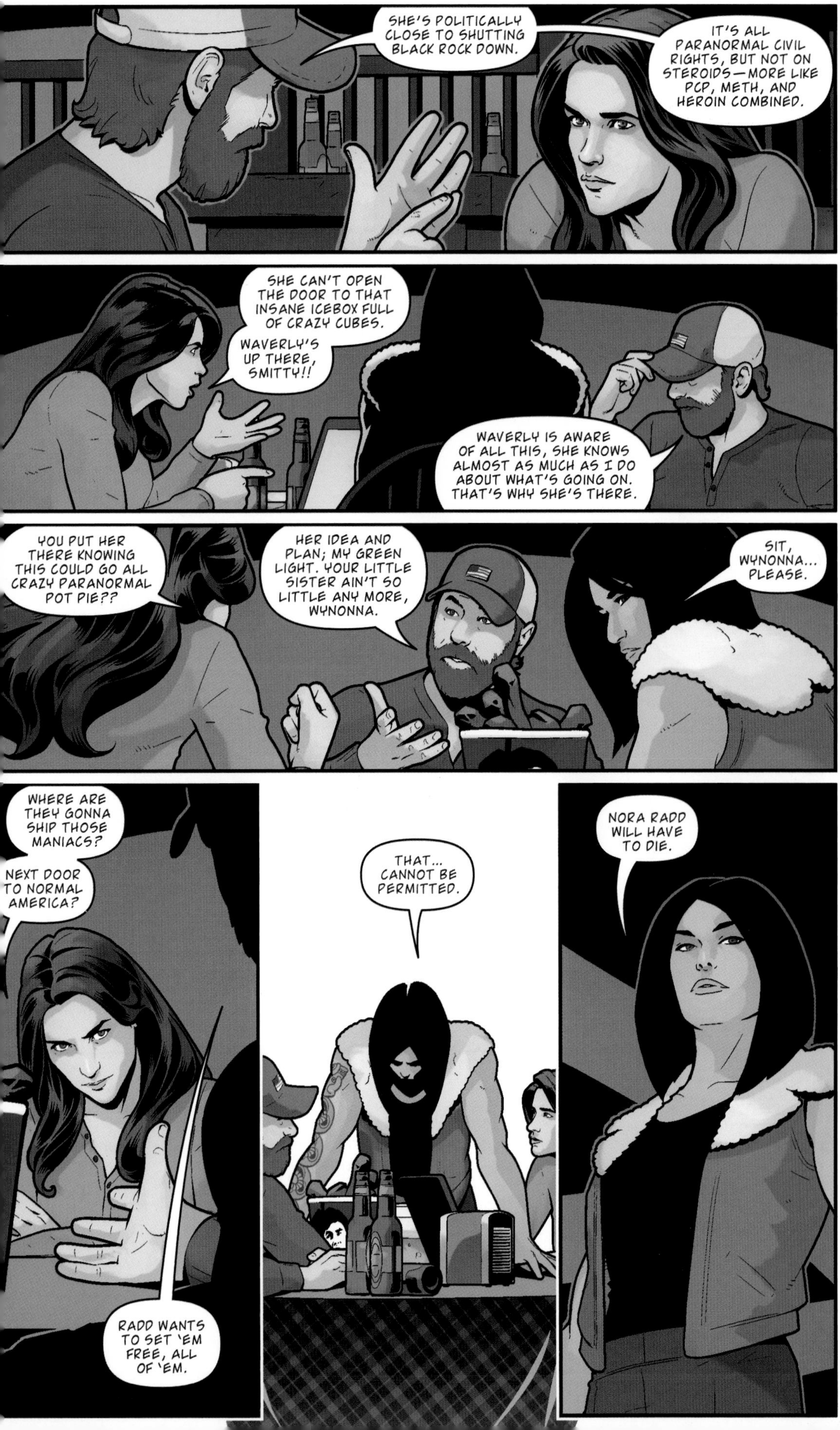
SHE'S POLITICALLY CLOSE TO SHUTTING BLACK ROCK DOWN.
IT'S ALL PARANORMAL CIVIL RIGHTS, BUT NOT ON STEROIDS—MORE LIKE PCP, METH, AND HEROIN COMBINED.
SHE CAN'T OPEN THE DOOR TO THAT INSANE ICEBOX FULL OF CRAZY CUBES.
WAVERLY'S UP THERE, SMITTY!!
WAVERLY IS AWARE OF ALL THIS, SHE KNOWS ALMOST AS MUCH AS I DO ABOUT WHAT'S GOING ON. THAT'S WHY SHE'S THERE.
YOU PUT HER THERE KNOWING THIS COULD GO ALL CRAZY PARANORMAL POT PIE??
HER IDEA AND PLAN; MY GREEN LIGHT. YOUR LITTLE SISTER AIN'T SO LITTLE ANY MORE, WYNONNA.
SIT, WYNONNA... PLEASE.
WHERE ARE THEY GONNA SHIP THOSE MANIACS?
NEXT DOOR TO NORMAL AMERICA?
RADD WANTS TO SET 'EM FREE, ALL OF 'EM.
THAT... CANNOT BE PERMITTED.
NORA RADD WILL HAVE TO DIE.

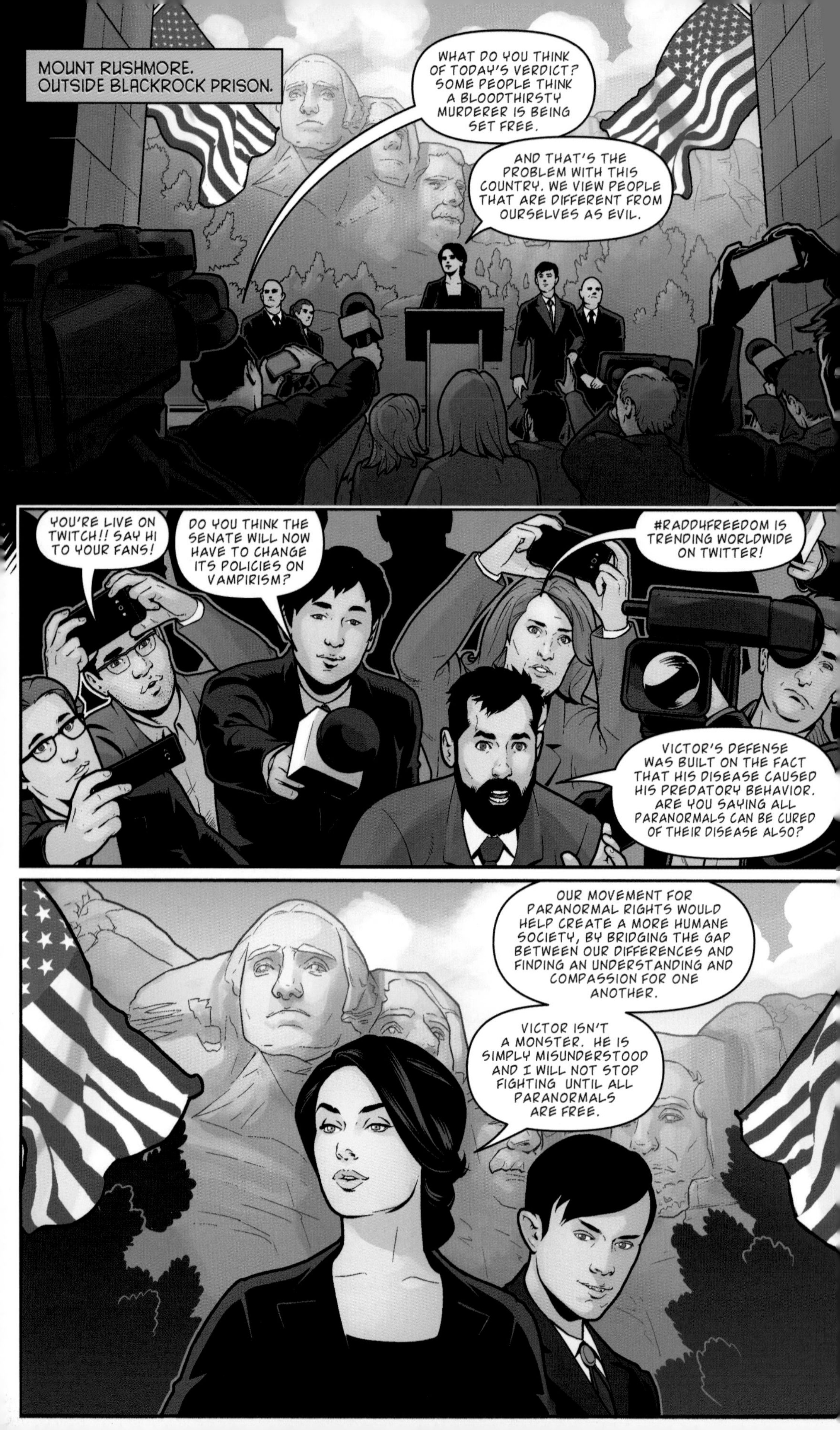

MOUNT RUSHMORE. OUTSIDE BLACKROCK PRISON.
WHAT DO YOU THINK OF TODAY'S VERDICT? SOME PEOPLE THINK A BLOODTHIRSTY MURDERER IS BEING SET FREE.
AND THAT'S THE PROBLEM WITH THIS COUNTRY. WE VIEW PEOPLE THAT ARE DIFFERENT FROM OURSELVES AS EVIL.
YOU'RE LIVE ON TWITCH!! SAY HI TO YOUR FANS!
DO YOU THINK THE SENATE WILL NOW HAVE TO CHANGE ITS POLICIES ON VAMPIRISM?
#RADD4FREEDOM IS TRENDING WORLDWIDE ON TWITTER!
VICTOR'S DEFENSE WAS BUILT ON THE FACT THAT HIS DISEASE CAUSED HIS PREDATORY BEHAVIOR. ARE YOU SAYING ALL PARANORMALS CAN BE CURED OF THEIR DISEASE ALSO?
OUR MOVEMENT FOR PARANORMAL RIGHTS WOULD HELP CREATE A MORE HUMANE SOCIETY, BY BRIDGING THE GAP BETWEEN OUR DIFFERENCES AND FINDING AN UNDERSTANDING AND COMPASSION FOR ONE ANOTHER.
VICTOR ISN'T A MONSTER. HE IS SIMPLY MISUNDERSTOOD AND I WILL NOT STOP FIGHTING UNTIL ALL PARANORMALS ARE FREE.

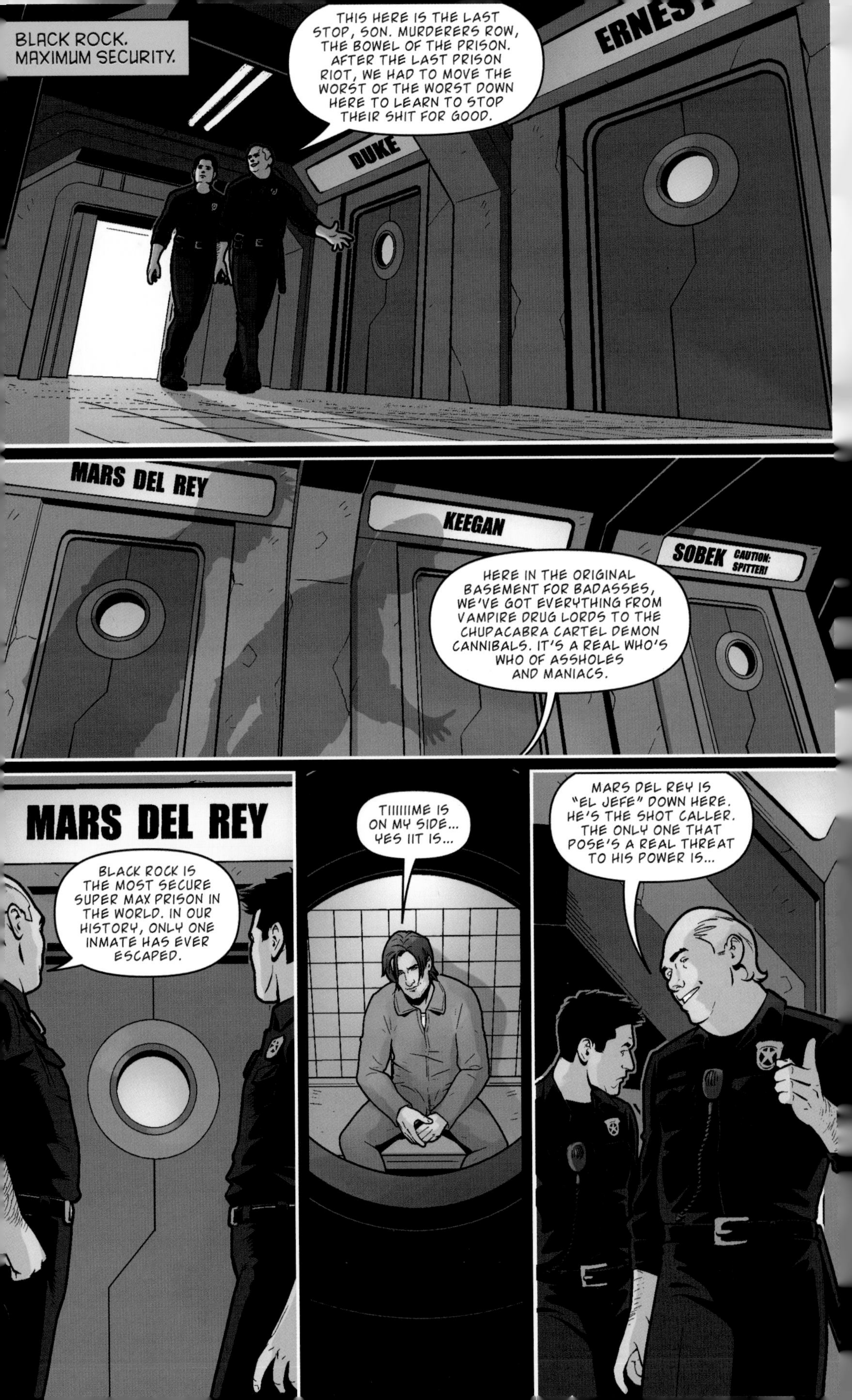
BLACK ROCK. MAXIMUM SECURITY.
THIS HERE IS THE LAST STOP, SON. MURDERERS ROW, THE BOWEL OF THE PRISON. AFTER THE LAST PRISON RIOT, WE HAD TO MOVE THE WORST OF THE WORST DOWN HERE TO LEARN TO STOP THEIR SHIT FOR GOOD.
DUKE
ERNEST
MARS DEL REY
KEEGAN
SOBEK CAUTION: SPITTER!
HERE IN THE ORIGINAL BASEMENT FOR BADASSES, WE'VE GOT EVERYTHING FROM VAMPIRE DRUG LORDS TO THE CHUPACABRA CARTEL DEMON CANNIBALS. IT'S A REAL WHO'S WHO OF ASSHOLES AND MANIACS.
MARS DEL REY
BLACK ROCK IS THE MOST SECURE SUPER MAX PRISON IN THE WORLD. IN OUR HISTORY, ONLY ONE INMATE HAS EVER ESCAPED.
TIIIIIIME IS ON MY SIDE... YES IIT IS...
MARS DEL REY IS "EL JEFE" DOWN HERE. HE'S THE SHOT CALLER. THE ONLY ONE THAT POSE'S A REAL THREAT TO HIS POWER IS...

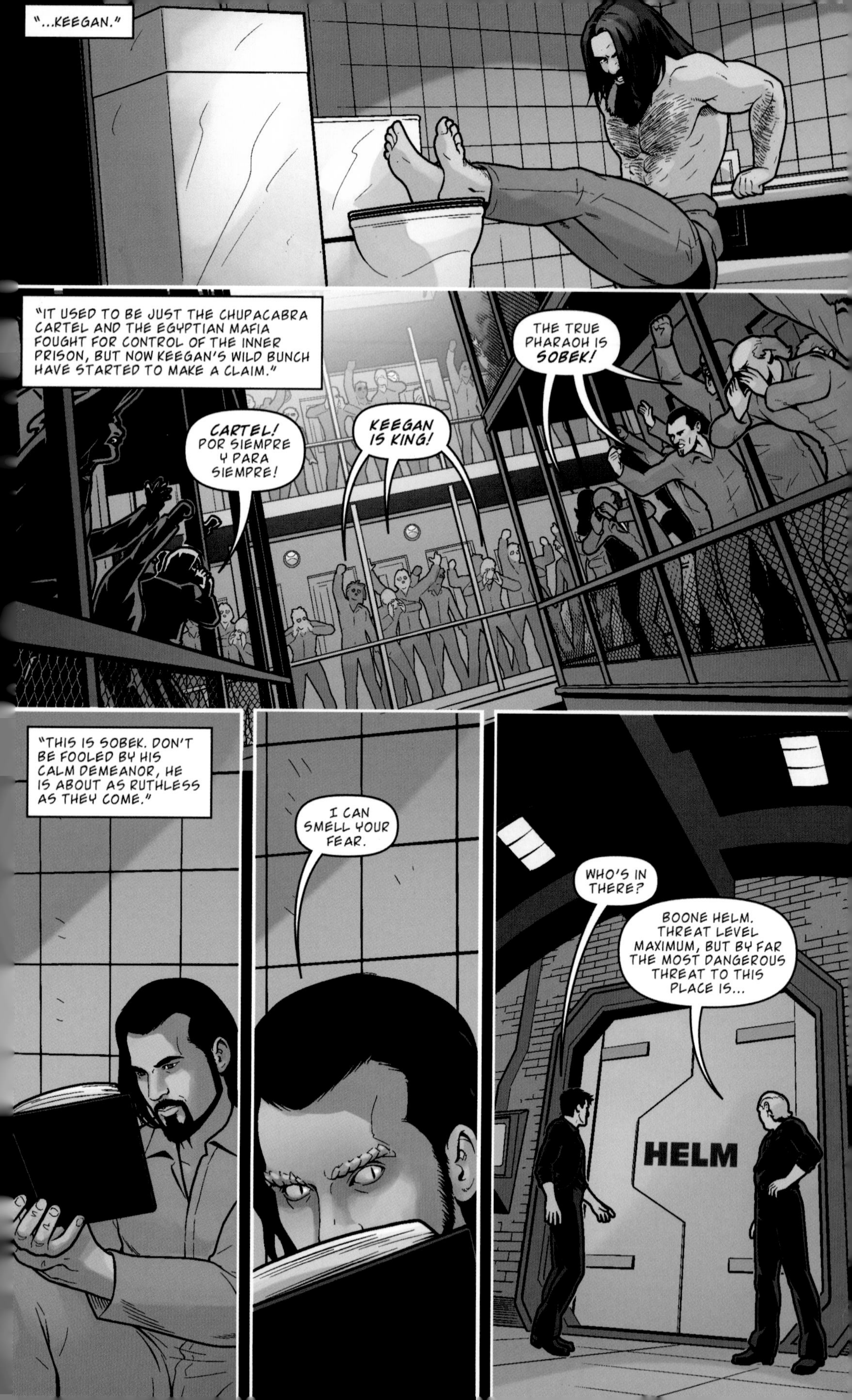
"...KEEGAN."
"IT USED TO BE JUST THE CHUPACABRA CARTEL AND THE EGYPTIAN MAFIA FOUGHT FOR CONTROL OF THE INNER PRISON, BUT NOW KEEGAN'S WILD BUNCH HAVE STARTED TO MAKE A CLAIM."
CARTEL! POR SIEMPRE Y PARA SIEMPRE!
KEEGAN IS KING!
THE TRUE PHARAOH IS SOBEK!
"THIS IS SOBEK. DON'T BE FOOLED BY HIS CALM DEMEANOR, HE IS ABOUT AS RUTHLESS AS THEY COME."
I CAN SMELL YOUR FEAR.
WHO'S IN THERE?
BOONE HELM. THREAT LEVEL MAXIMUM, BUT BY FAR THE MOST DANGEROUS THREAT TO THIS PLACE IS...
HELM

"...THEM."

MOUNT RUSHMORE

Not Normal / Ot Natural / lot Here!

NOT GOOD

NORA RADD: RADI[C]ALLY WE

NORA RADD FOR PRESIDENT

[F]REEDOM 4 PARA NORMALS

MY SON WAS KILLED BY THAT BLOOD-SUCKING MONSTER!!

NORA RADD FOR [PR]ESIDENT

YOUR SON NEVER HAD TO GROW UP BEING CALLED A MONSTER!!

PARANORMAL NOT PARAMILITARY!

WAVERLY, DO YOU COPY? I THINK THINGS ARE ABOUT TO GET UGLY.

YOU'RE IN MY EAR! I LOVE YOUR SHIRT BY THE WAY. I WISH EVERYONE WOULD JUST GET ALONG. I WISH THEY WOULD JUST LISTEN TO EACH OTHER!

SOMETIMES THINGS JUST NEED TO GET WORSE BEFORE THEY CAN GET BETTER. I THINK WE SHOULD CALL WYNONNA.

Freedom For All Not The Sel...

YOU'RE SUPPORTING KILLERS!!!

[ST]OP THE [W]ITCH HUNT!

SET THEM FREE!!!

GET BACK TO THE BASE IMMEDIATELY, NICOLE!! I THINK THINGS ARE ABOUT TO GET REALLY BAD!!

OH, SHIT.

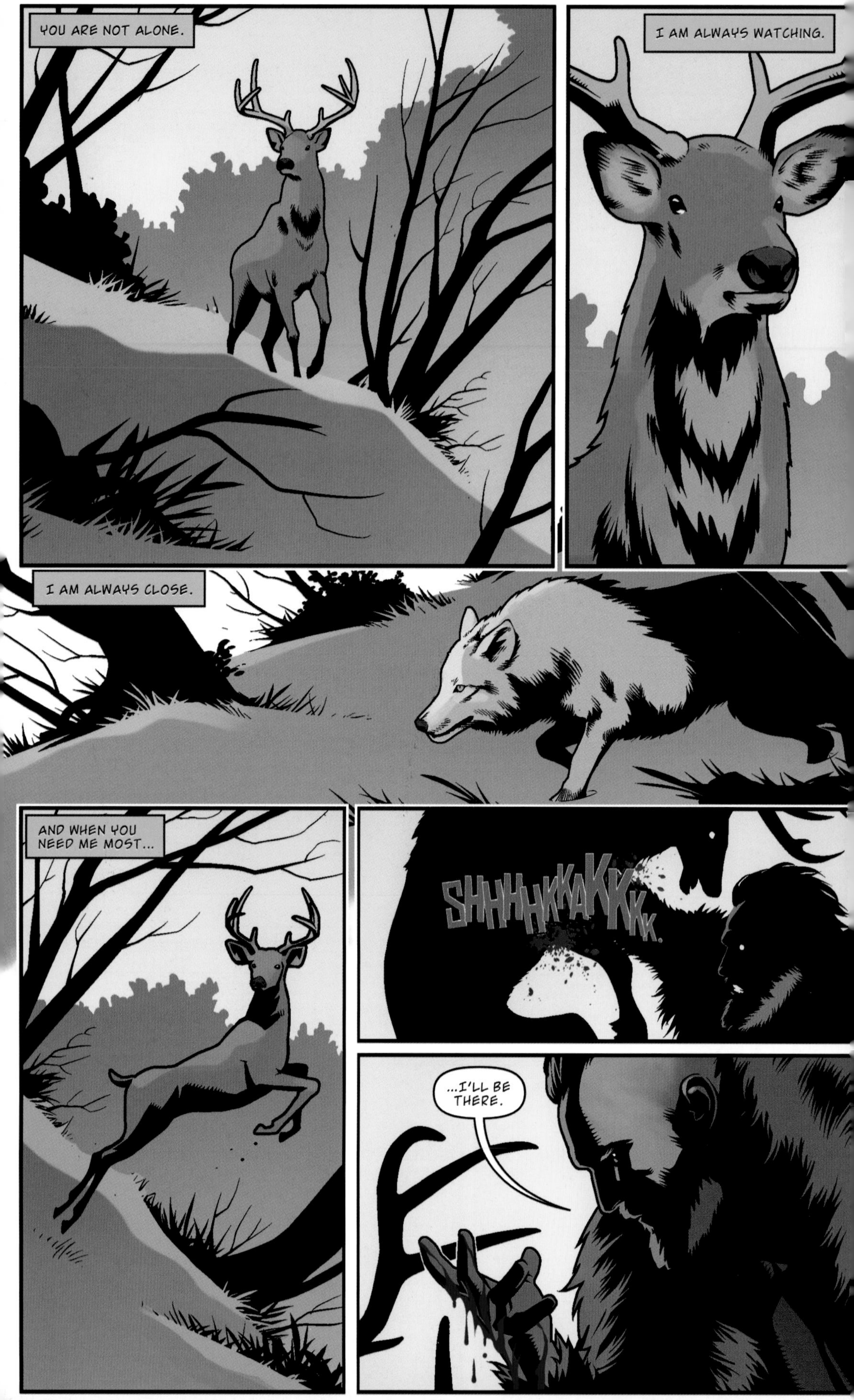
YOU ARE NOT ALONE.
I AM ALWAYS WATCHING.
I AM ALWAYS CLOSE.
AND WHEN YOU NEED ME MOST...
SHHHHKKAKKKk.
...I'LL BE THERE.

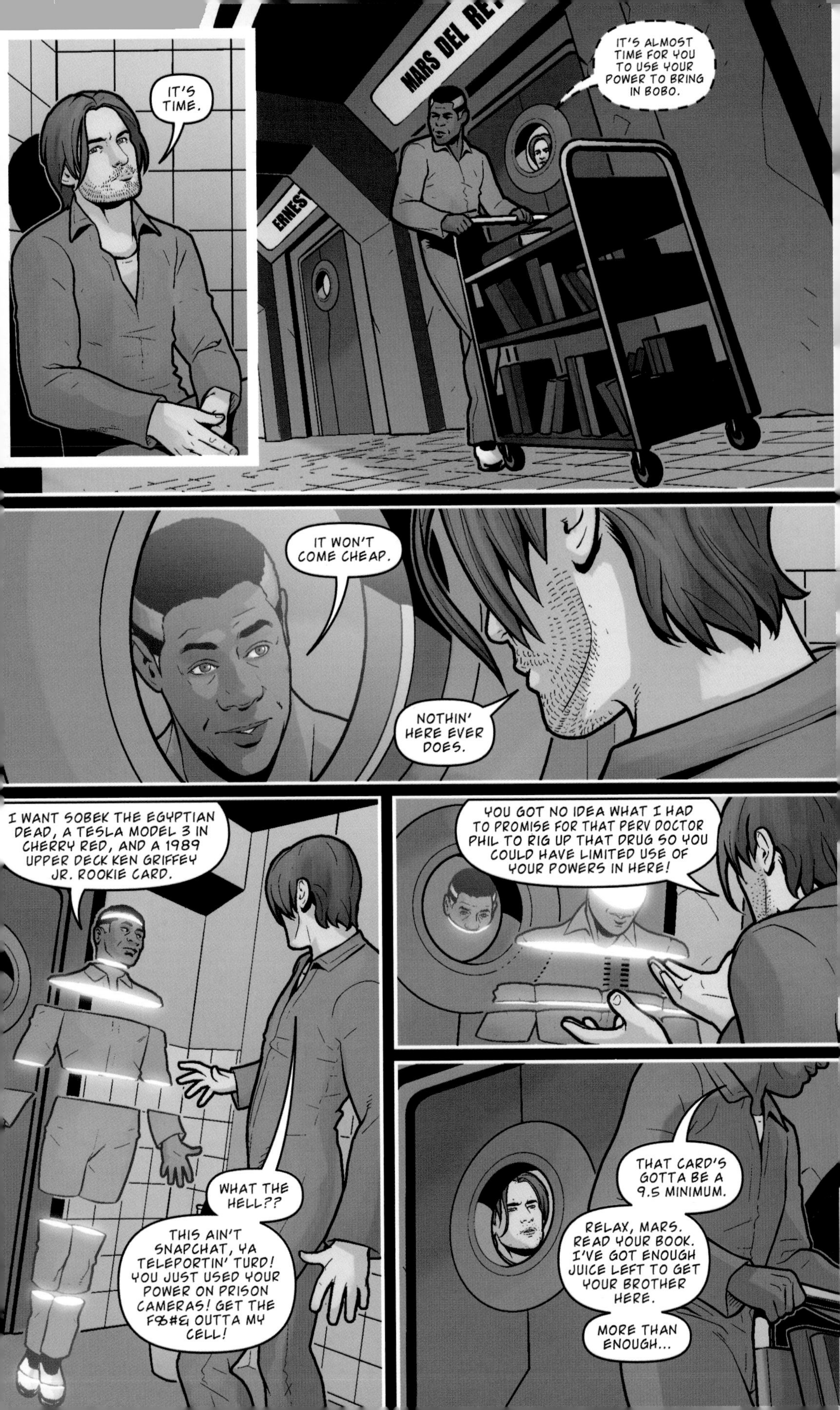
IT'S TIME.
MARS DEL RE
ERNEST
IT'S ALMOST TIME FOR YOU TO USE YOUR POWER TO BRING IN BOBO.
IT WON'T COME CHEAP.
NOTHIN' HERE EVER DOES.
I WANT SOBEK THE EGYPTIAN DEAD, A TESLA MODEL 3 IN CHERRY RED, AND A 1989 UPPER DECK KEN GRIFFEY JR. ROOKIE CARD.
WHAT THE HELL??
THIS AIN'T SNAPCHAT, YA TELEPORTIN' TURD! YOU JUST USED YOUR POWER ON PRISON CAMERAS! GET THE F&#& OUTTA MY CELL!
YOU GOT NO IDEA WHAT I HAD TO PROMISE FOR THAT PERV DOCTOR PHIL TO RIG UP THAT DRUG SO YOU COULD HAVE LIMITED USE OF YOUR POWERS IN HERE!
THAT CARD'S GOTTA BE A 9.5 MINIMUM.
RELAX, MARS. READ YOUR BOOK. I'VE GOT ENOUGH JUICE LEFT TO GET YOUR BROTHER HERE.
MORE THAN ENOUGH...

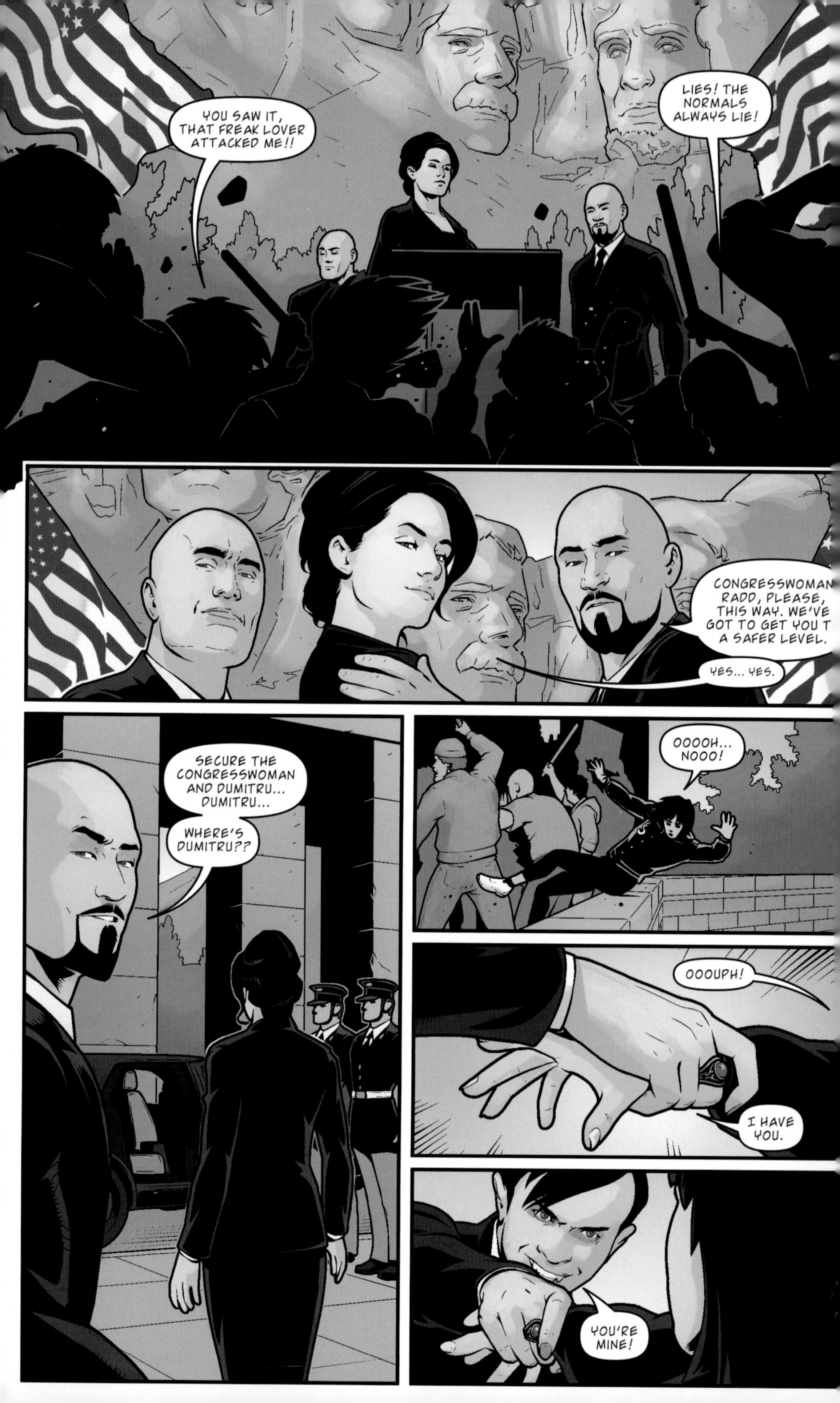
YOU SAW IT, THAT FREAK LOVER ATTACKED ME!!
LIES! THE NORMALS ALWAYS LIE!
CONGRESSWOMAN RADD, PLEASE, THIS WAY. WE'VE GOT TO GET YOU T A SAFER LEVEL.
YES... YES.
SECURE THE CONGRESSWOMAN AND DUMITRU... DUMITRU...
WHERE'S DUMITRU??
OOOOH... NOOO!
OOOUPH!
I HAVE YOU.
YOU'RE MINE!

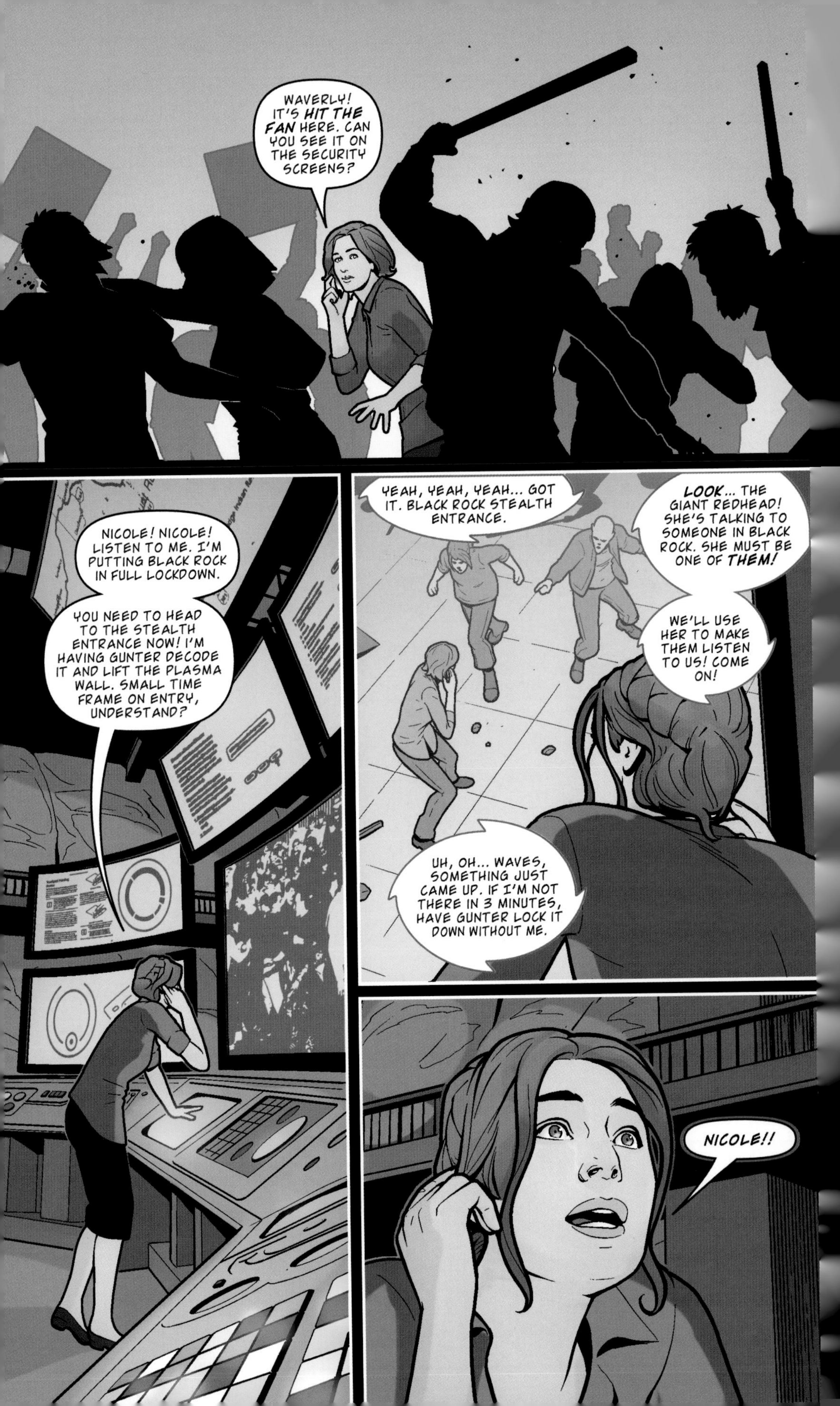

WAVERLY! IT'S HIT THE FAN HERE. CAN YOU SEE IT ON THE SECURITY SCREENS?
NICOLE! NICOLE! LISTEN TO ME. I'M PUTTING BLACK ROCK IN FULL LOCKDOWN.
YOU NEED TO HEAD TO THE STEALTH ENTRANCE NOW! I'M HAVING GUNTER DECODE IT AND LIFT THE PLASMA WALL. SMALL TIME FRAME ON ENTRY, UNDERSTAND?
YEAH, YEAH, YEAH... GOT IT. BLACK ROCK STEALTH ENTRANCE.
LOOK... THE GIANT REDHEAD! SHE'S TALKING TO SOMEONE IN BLACK ROCK. SHE MUST BE ONE OF THEM!
WE'LL USE HER TO MAKE THEM LISTEN TO US! COME ON!
UH, OH... WAVES, SOMETHING JUST CAME UP. IF I'M NOT THERE IN 3 MINUTES, HAVE GUNTER LOCK IT DOWN WITHOUT ME.
NICOLE!!

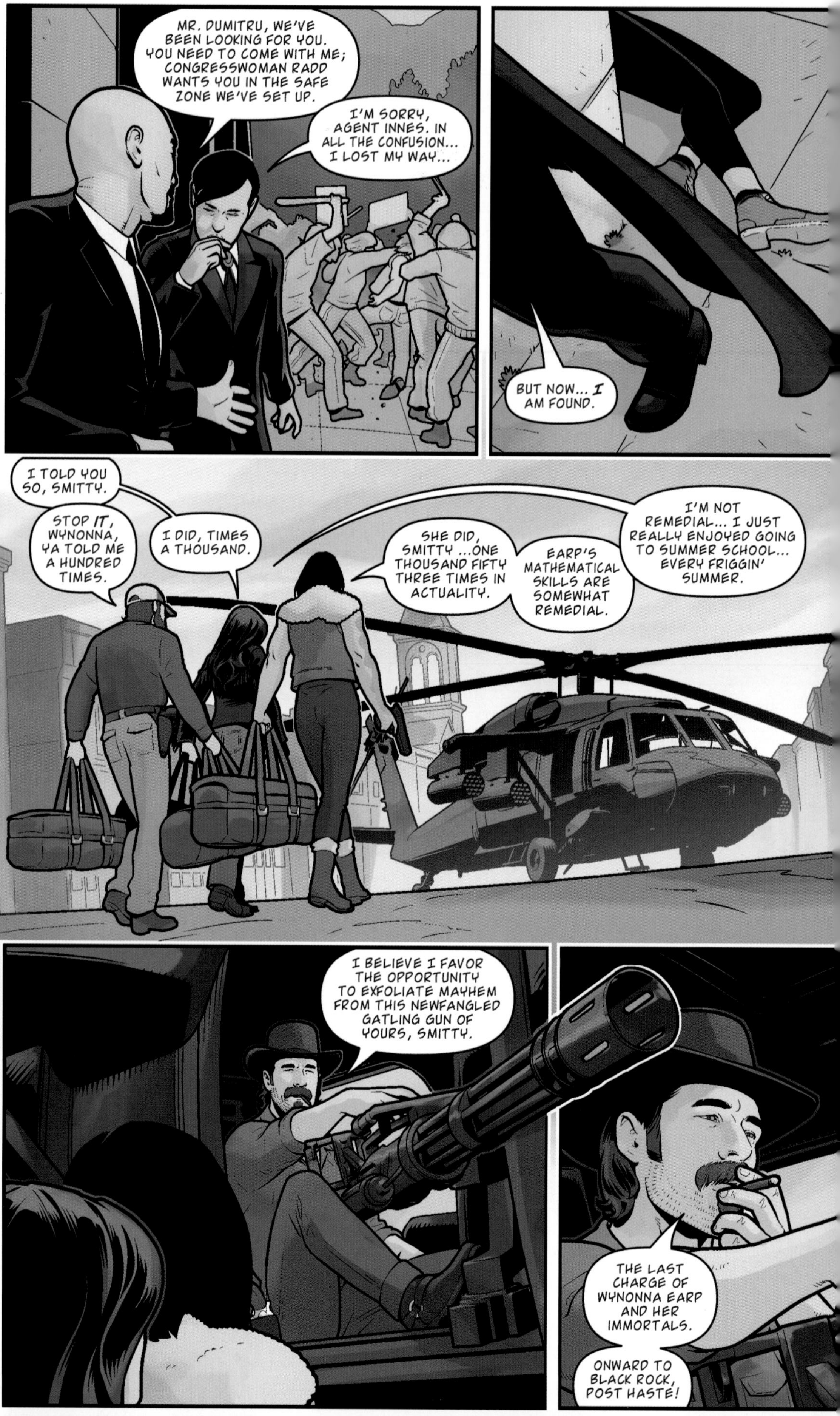
MR. DUMITRU, WE'VE BEEN LOOKING FOR YOU. YOU NEED TO COME WITH ME; CONGRESSWOMAN RADD WANTS YOU IN THE SAFE ZONE WE'VE SET UP.
I'M SORRY, AGENT INNES. IN ALL THE CONFUSION... I LOST MY WAY...
BUT NOW... I AM FOUND.
I TOLD YOU SO, SMITTY.
STOP IT, WYNONNA, YA TOLD ME A HUNDRED TIMES.
I DID, TIMES A THOUSAND.
SHE DID, SMITTY ...ONE THOUSAND FIFTY THREE TIMES IN ACTUALITY.
EARP'S MATHEMATICAL SKILLS ARE SOMEWHAT REMEDIAL.
I'M NOT REMEDIAL... I JUST REALLY ENJOYED GOING TO SUMMER SCHOOL... EVERY FRIGGIN' SUMMER.
I BELIEVE I FAVOR THE OPPORTUNITY TO EXFOLIATE MAYHEM FROM THIS NEWFANGLED GATLING GUN OF YOURS, SMITTY.
THE LAST CHARGE OF WYNONNA EARP AND HER IMMORTALS.
ONWARD TO BLACK ROCK, POST HASTE!

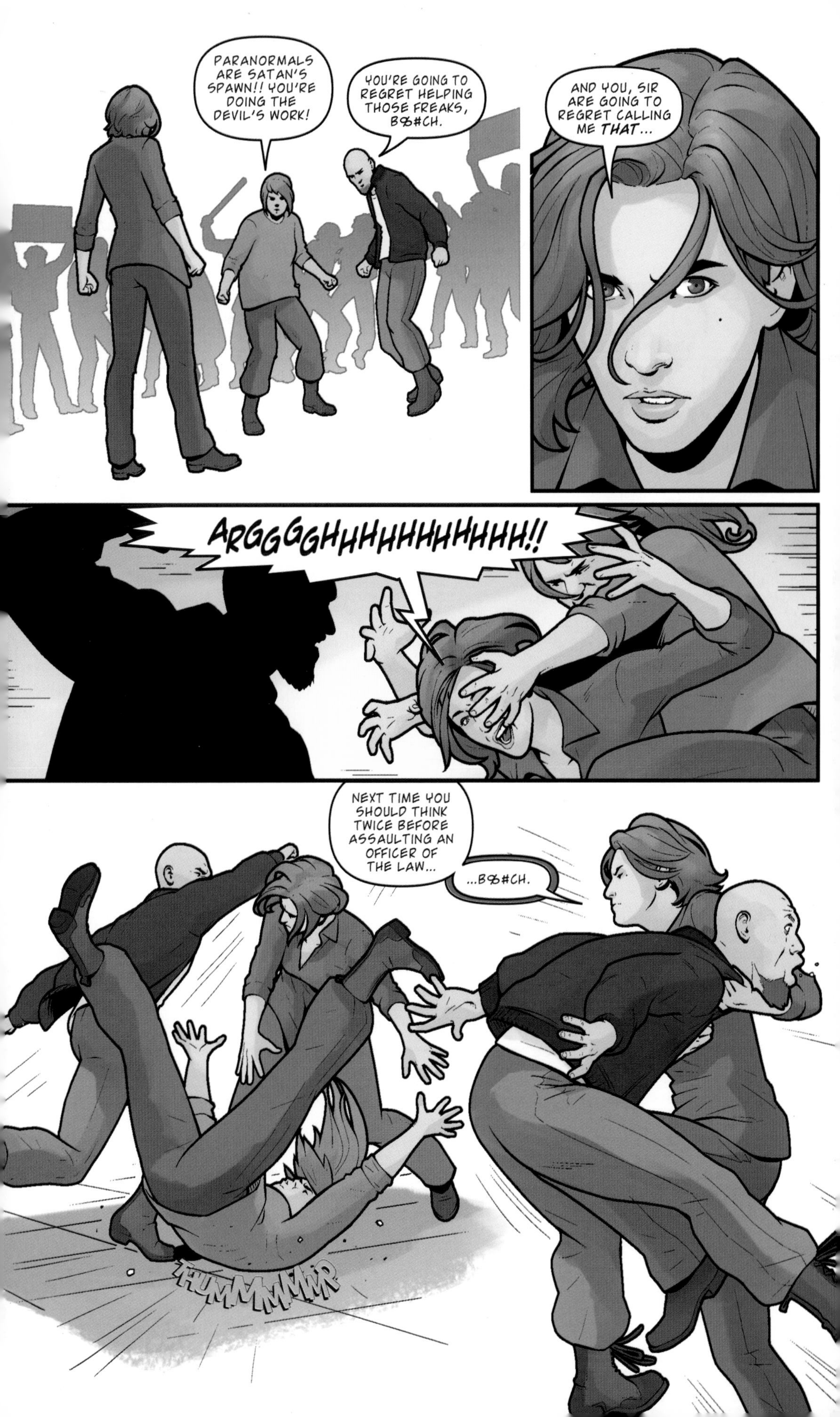
PARANORMALS ARE SATAN'S SPAWN!! YOU'RE DOING THE DEVIL'S WORK!
YOU'RE GOING TO REGRET HELPING THOSE FREAKS, B%#CH.
AND YOU, SIR ARE GOING TO REGRET CALLING ME *THAT*...
ARGGGGHHHHHHHHHH!!
NEXT TIME YOU SHOULD THINK TWICE BEFORE ASSAULTING AN OFFICER OF THE LAW...
...B%#CH.
THUMMMMMP

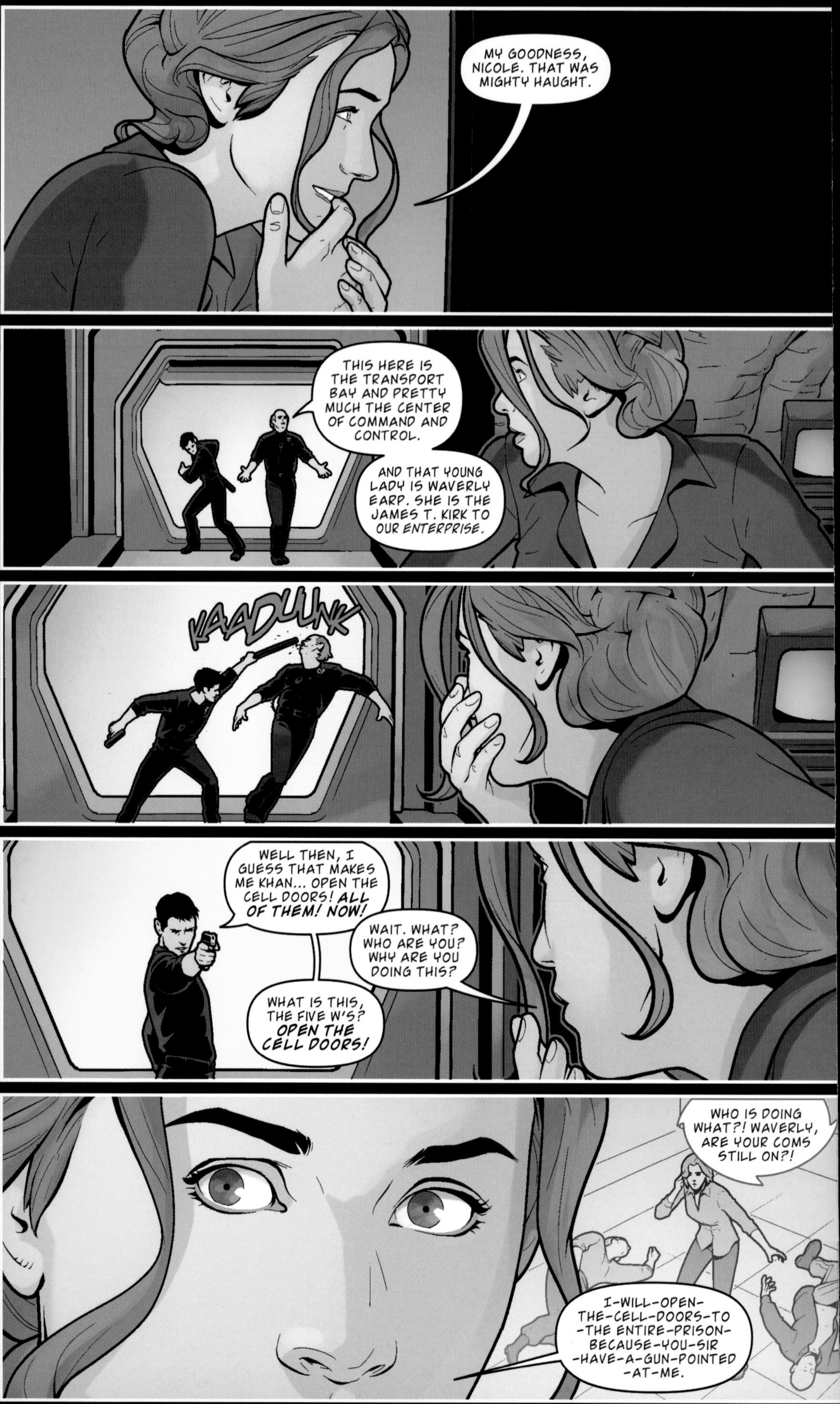

MY GOODNESS, NICOLE. THAT WAS MIGHTY HAUGHT.
THIS HERE IS THE TRANSPORT BAY AND PRETTY MUCH THE CENTER OF COMMAND AND CONTROL.
AND THAT YOUNG LADY IS WAVERLY EARP. SHE IS THE JAMES T. KIRK TO OUR *ENTERPRISE*.
KAADUUNK
WELL THEN, I GUESS THAT MAKES ME KHAN... OPEN THE CELL DOORS! ***ALL OF THEM! NOW!***
WAIT. WHAT? WHO ARE YOU? WHY ARE YOU DOING THIS?
WHAT IS THIS, THE FIVE W'S? ***OPEN THE CELL DOORS!***
WHO IS DOING WHAT?! WAVERLY, ARE YOUR COMS STILL ON?!
I-WILL-OPEN-THE-CELL-DOORS-TO-THE ENTIRE-PRISON-BECAUSE-YOU-SIR-HAVE-A-GUN-POINTED-AT-ME.

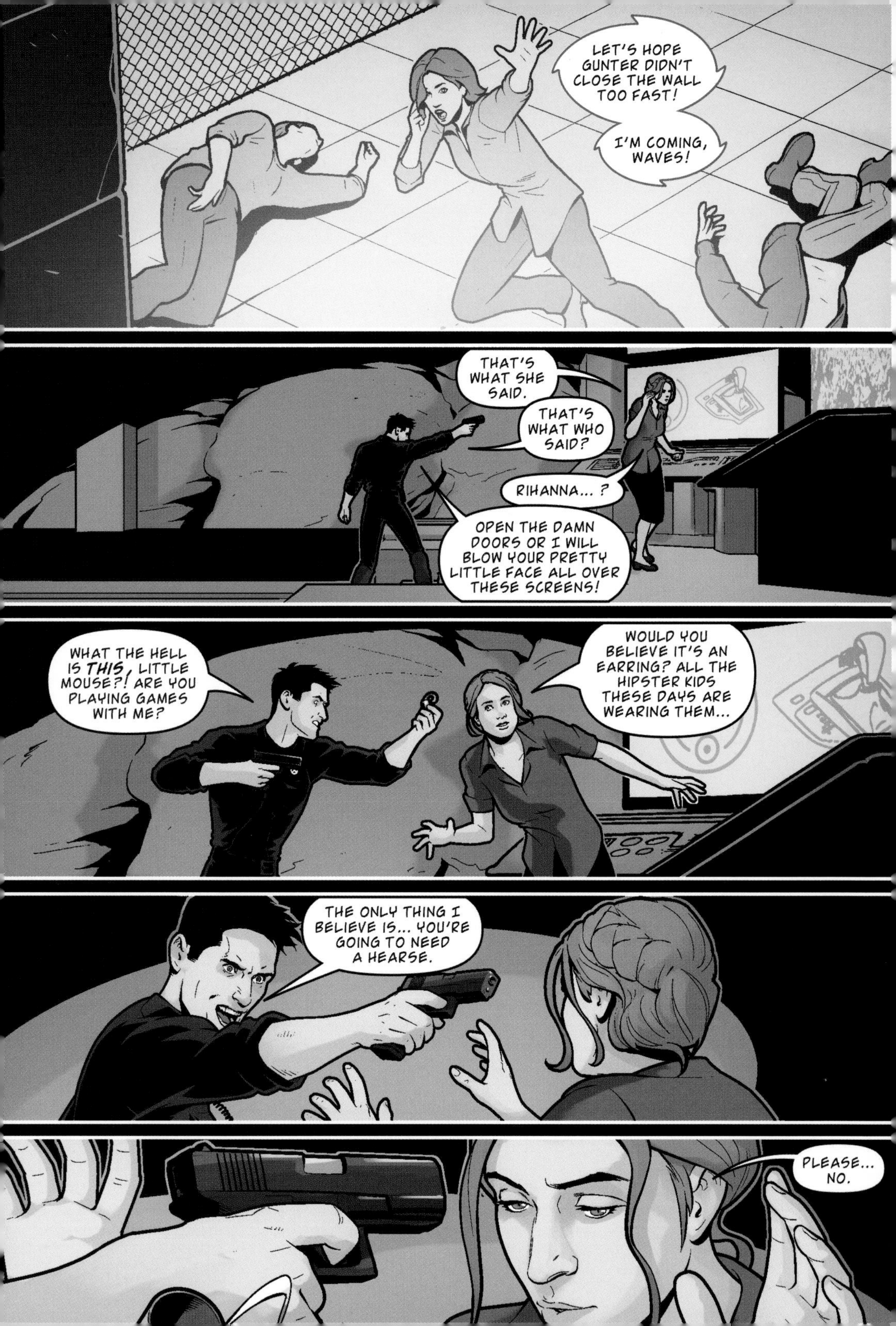
LET'S HOPE GUNTER DIDN'T CLOSE THE WALL TOO FAST!
I'M COMING, WAVES!
THAT'S WHAT SHE SAID.
THAT'S WHAT WHO SAID?
RIHANNA... ?
OPEN THE DAMN DOORS OR I WILL BLOW YOUR PRETTY LITTLE FACE ALL OVER THESE SCREENS!
WHAT THE HELL IS *THIS*, LITTLE MOUSE?! ARE YOU PLAYING GAMES WITH ME?
WOULD YOU BELIEVE IT'S AN EARRING? ALL THE HIPSTER KIDS THESE DAYS ARE WEARING THEM...
THE ONLY THING I BELIEVE IS... YOU'RE GOING TO NEED A HEARSE.
PLEASE... NO.

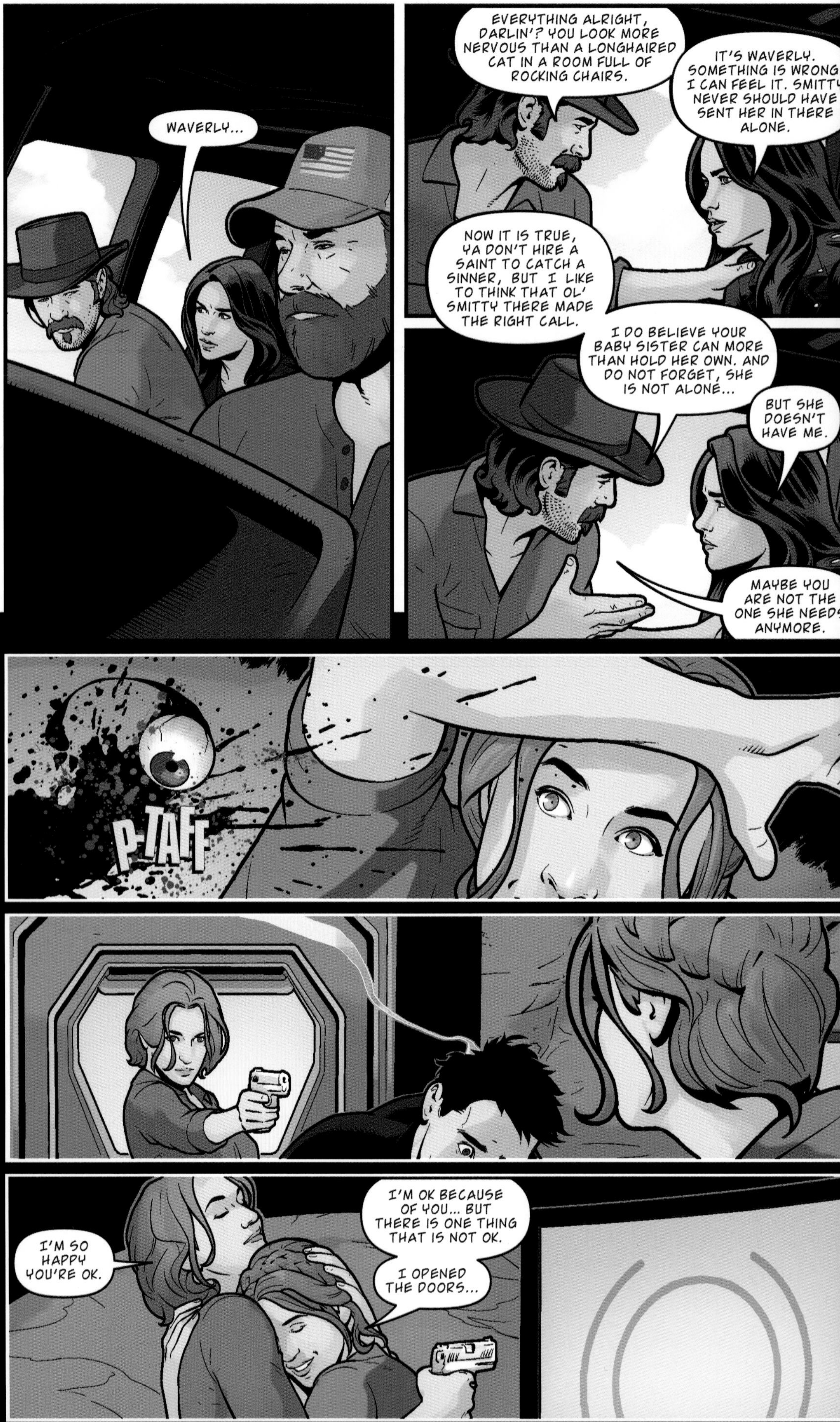

WAVERLY...
EVERYTHING ALRIGHT, DARLIN'? YOU LOOK MORE NERVOUS THAN A LONGHAIRED CAT IN A ROOM FULL OF ROCKING CHAIRS.
IT'S WAVERLY. SOMETHING IS WRONG. I CAN FEEL IT. SMITTY NEVER SHOULD HAVE SENT HER IN THERE ALONE.
NOW IT IS TRUE, YA DON'T HIRE A SAINT TO CATCH A SINNER, BUT I LIKE TO THINK THAT OL' SMITTY THERE MADE THE RIGHT CALL.
I DO BELIEVE YOUR BABY SISTER CAN MORE THAN HOLD HER OWN. AND DO NOT FORGET, SHE IS NOT ALONE...
BUT SHE DOESN'T HAVE ME.
MAYBE YOU ARE NOT THE ONE SHE NEEDS ANYMORE.
P-TAFF
I'M SO HAPPY YOU'RE OK.
I'M OK BECAUSE OF YOU... BUT THERE IS ONE THING THAT IS NOT OK.
I OPENED THE DOORS...

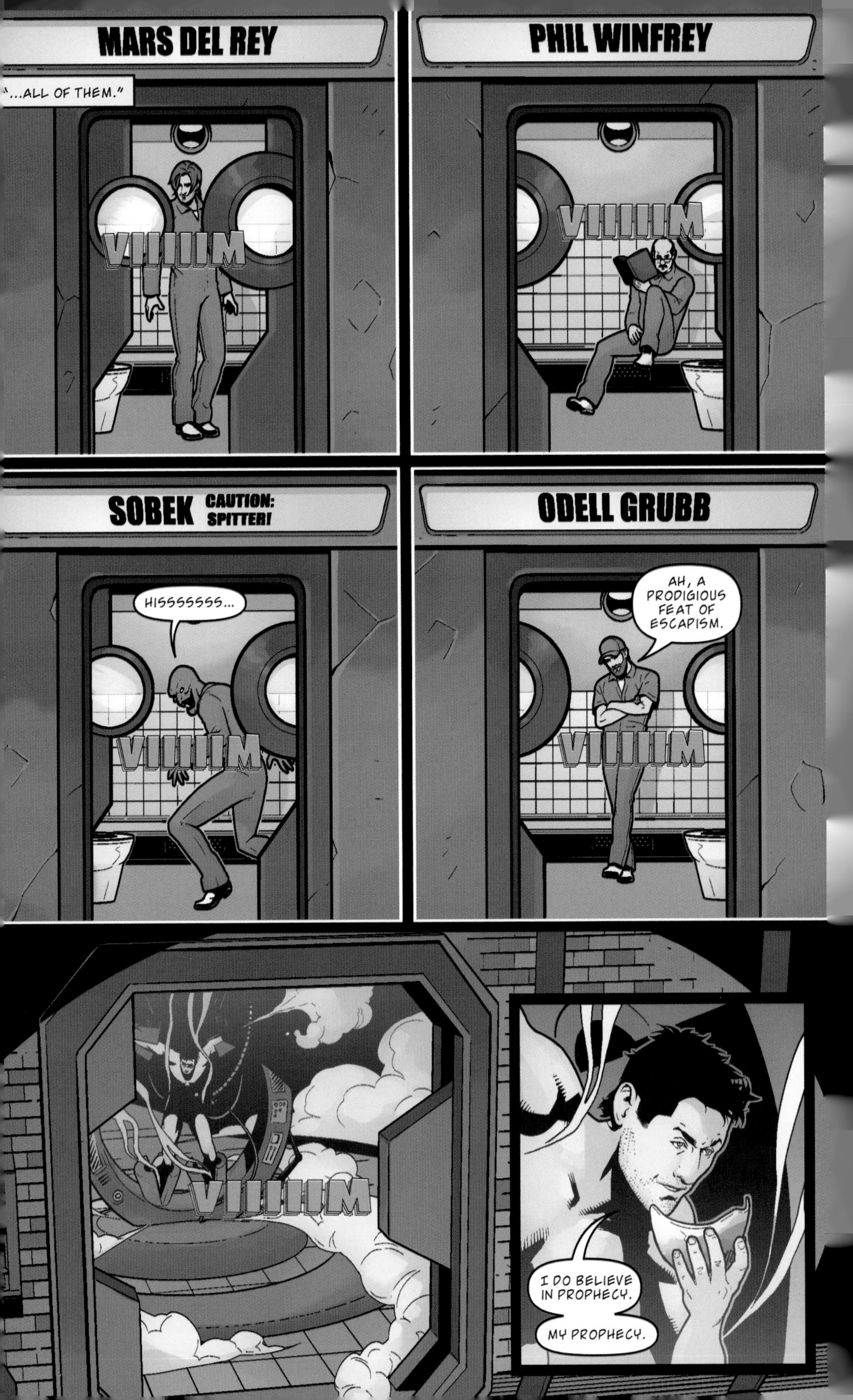
MARS DEL REY
"...ALL OF THEM."
VIIIIIM
PHIL WINFREY
VIIIIIIM
SOBEK
CAUTION: SPITTER!
HISSSSSSS...
VIIIIIM
ODELL GRUBB
AH, A PRODIGIOUS FEAT OF ESCAPISM.
VIIIIIM
VIIIIIM
I DO BELIEVE IN PROPHECY.
MY PROPHECY.

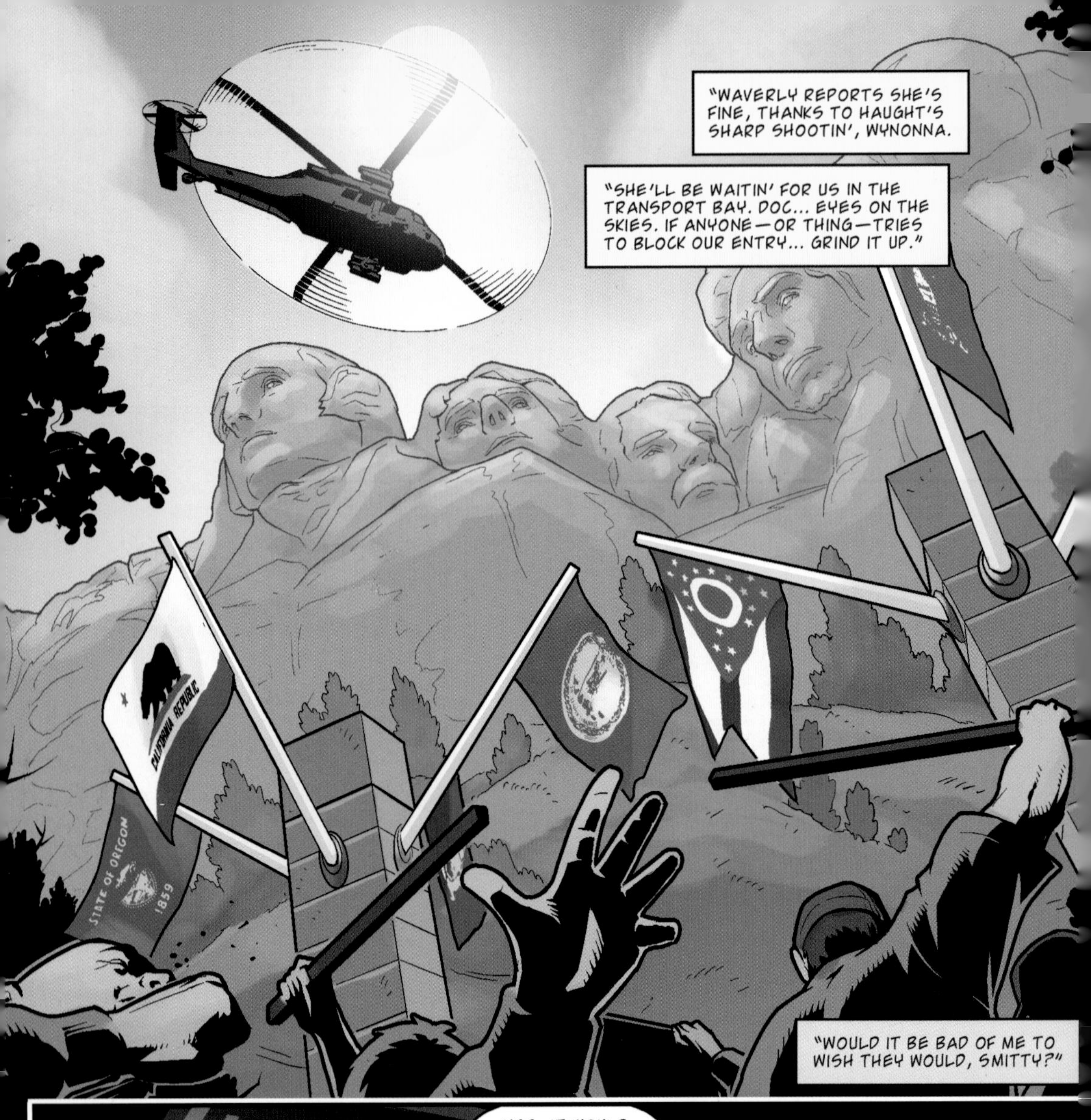
"WAVERLY REPORTS SHE'S FINE, THANKS TO HAUGHT'S SHARP SHOOTIN', WYNONNA.
"SHE'LL BE WAITIN' FOR US IN THE TRANSPORT BAY. DOC... EYES ON THE SKIES. IF ANYONE—OR THING—TRIES TO BLOCK OUR ENTRY... GRIND IT UP."
CALIFORNIA REPUBLIC
STATE OF OREGON 1859
"WOULD IT BE BAD OF ME TO WISH THEY WOULD, SMITTY?"

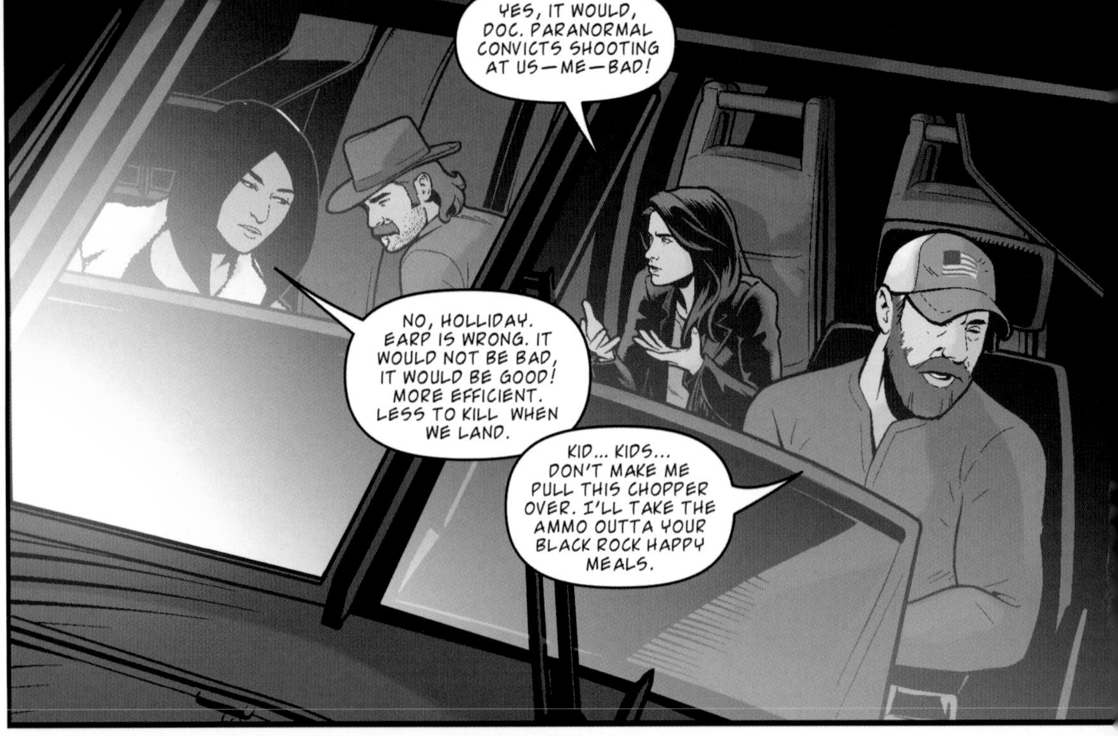
YES, IT WOULD, DOC. PARANORMAL CONVICTS SHOOTING AT US—ME—BAD!
NO, HOLLIDAY. EARP IS WRONG. IT WOULD NOT BE BAD, IT WOULD BE GOOD! MORE EFFICIENT. LESS TO KILL WHEN WE LAND.
KID... KIDS... DON'T MAKE ME PULL THIS CHOPPER OVER. I'LL TAKE THE AMMO OUTTA YOUR BLACK ROCK HAPPY MEALS.

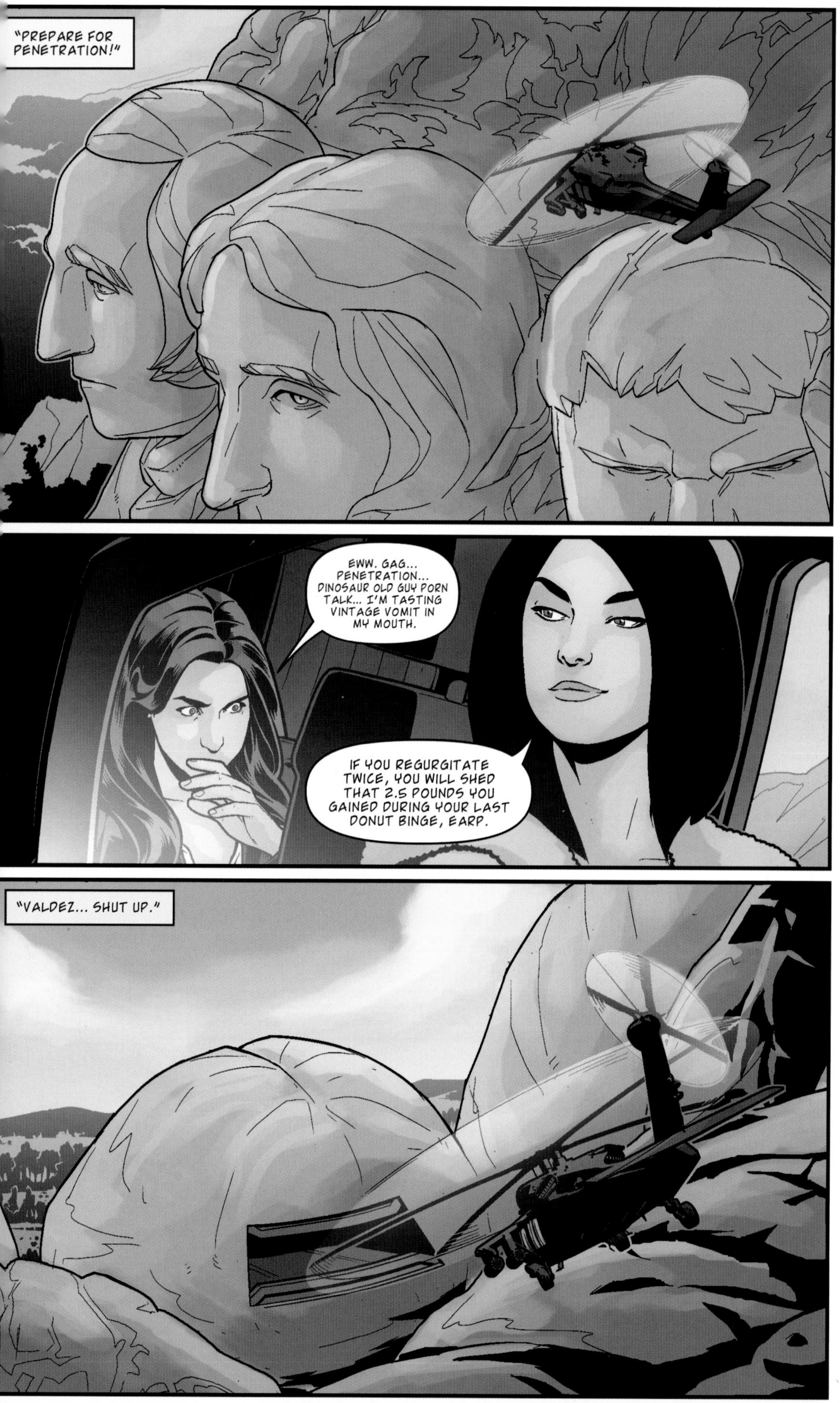

"PREPARE FOR PENETRATION!"
EWW. GAG... PENETRATION... DINOSAUR OLD GUY PORN TALK... I'M TASTING VINTAGE VOMIT IN MY MOUTH.
IF YOU REGURGITATE TWICE, YOU WILL SHED THAT 2.5 POUNDS YOU GAINED DURING YOUR LAST DONUT BINGE, EARP.
"VALDEZ... SHUT UP."

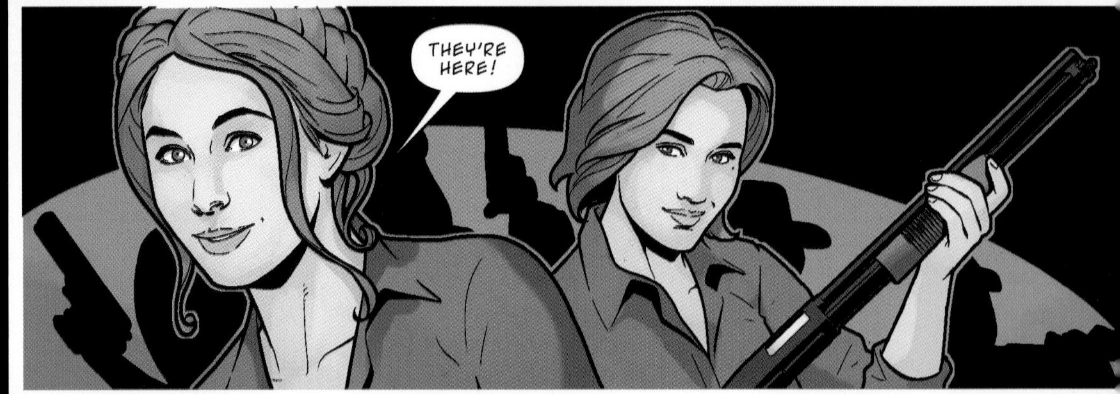
THEY'RE HERE!

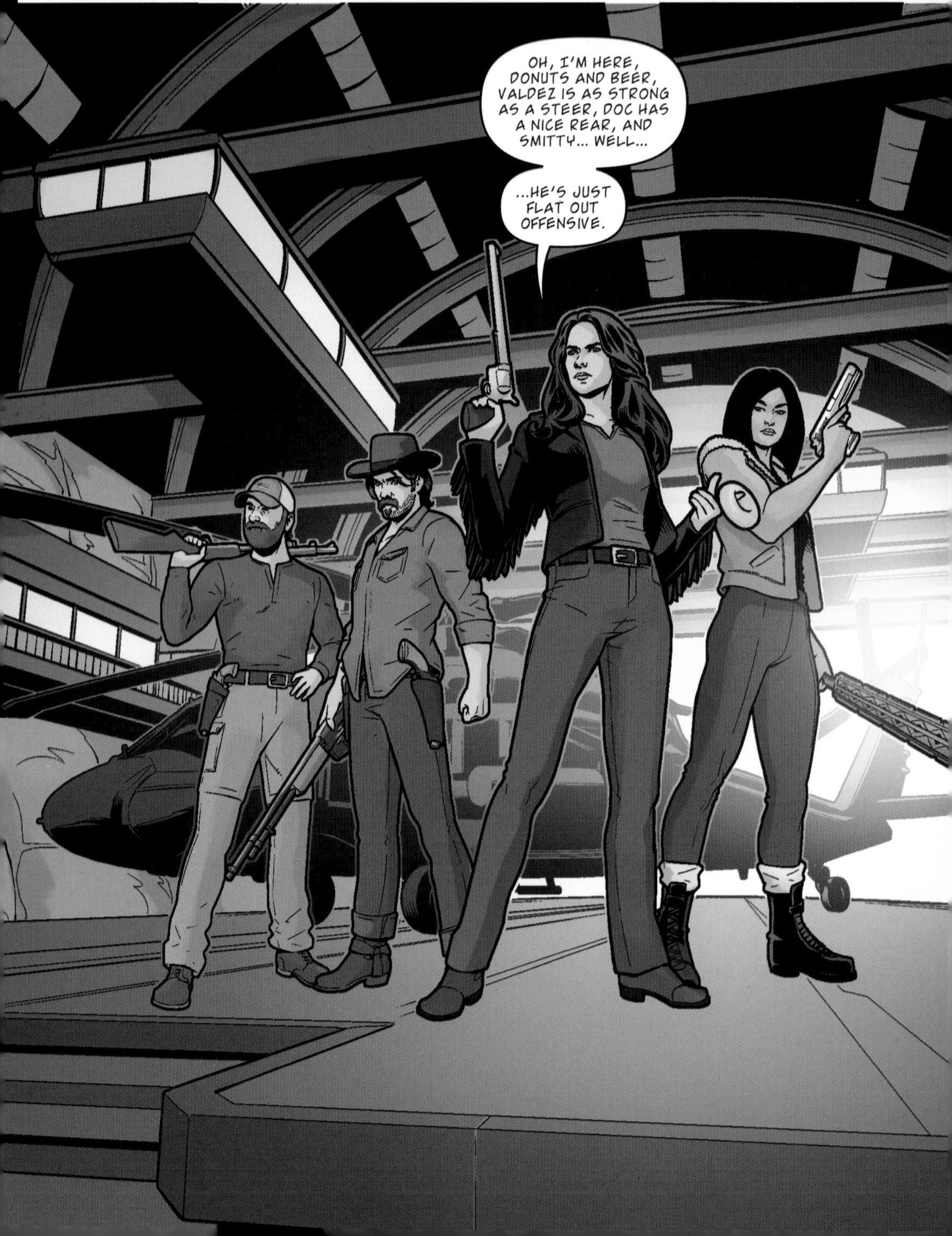
OH, I'M HERE, DONUTS AND BEER, VALDEZ IS AS STRONG AS A STEER, DOC HAS A NICE REAR, AND SMITTY... WELL...
...HE'S JUST FLAT OUT OFFENSIVE.

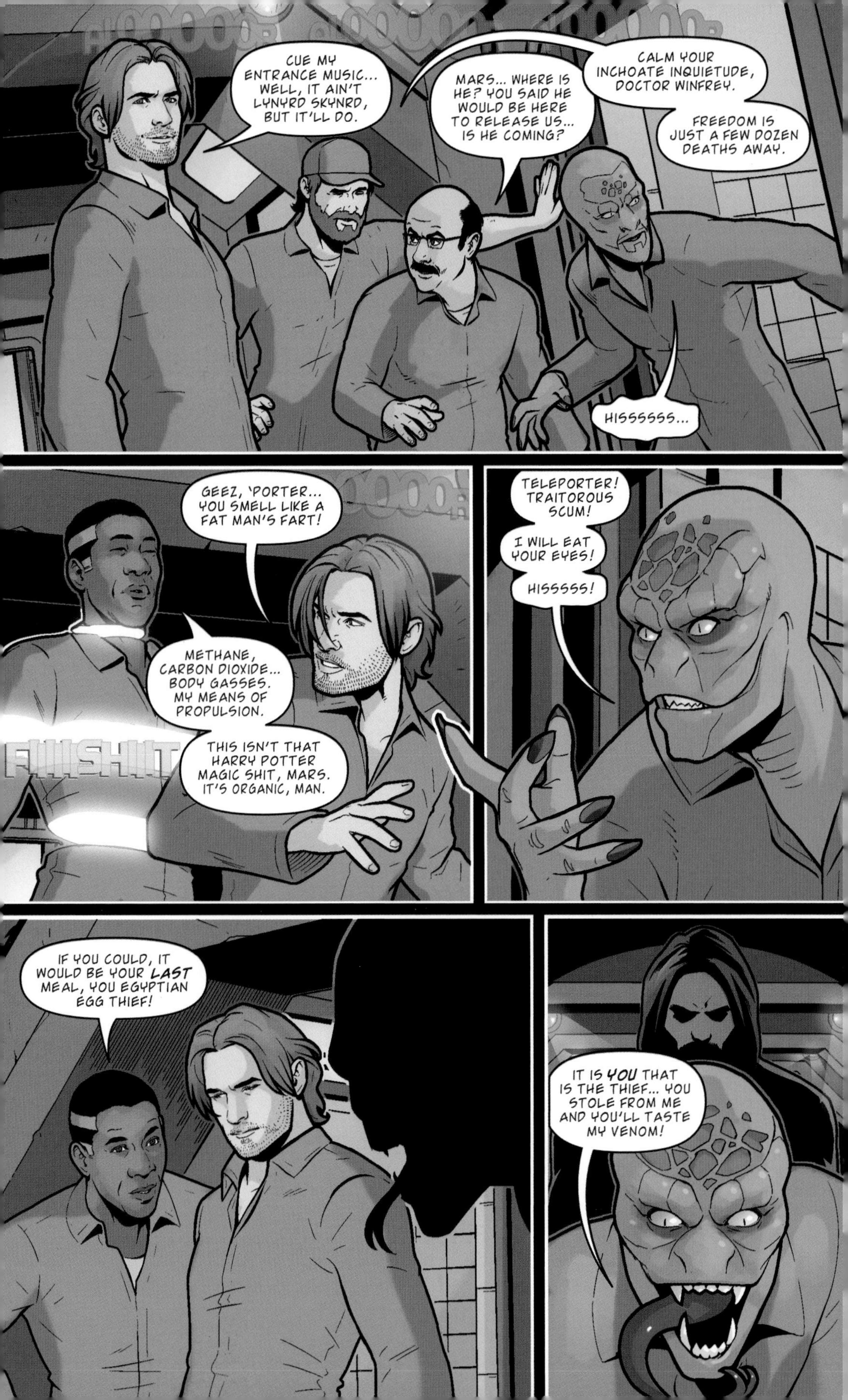
CUE MY ENTRANCE MUSIC... WELL, IT AIN'T LYNYRD SKYNRD, BUT IT'LL DO.
MARS... WHERE IS HE? YOU SAID HE WOULD BE HERE TO RELEASE US... IS HE COMING?
CALM YOUR INCHOATE INQUIETUDE, DOCTOR WINFREY.
FREEDOM IS JUST A FEW DOZEN DEATHS AWAY.
HISSSSSS...
FIIISHIT
GEEZ, 'PORTER... YOU SMELL LIKE A FAT MAN'S FART!
METHANE, CARBON DIOXIDE... BODY GASSES. MY MEANS OF PROPULSION.
THIS ISN'T THAT HARRY POTTER MAGIC SHIT, MARS. IT'S ORGANIC, MAN.
TELEPORTER! TRAITOROUS SCUM!
I WILL EAT YOUR EYES!
HISSSSS!
IF YOU COULD, IT WOULD BE YOUR LAST MEAL, YOU EGYPTIAN EGG THIEF!
IT IS YOU THAT IS THE THIEF... YOU STOLE FROM ME AND YOU'LL TASTE MY VENOM!

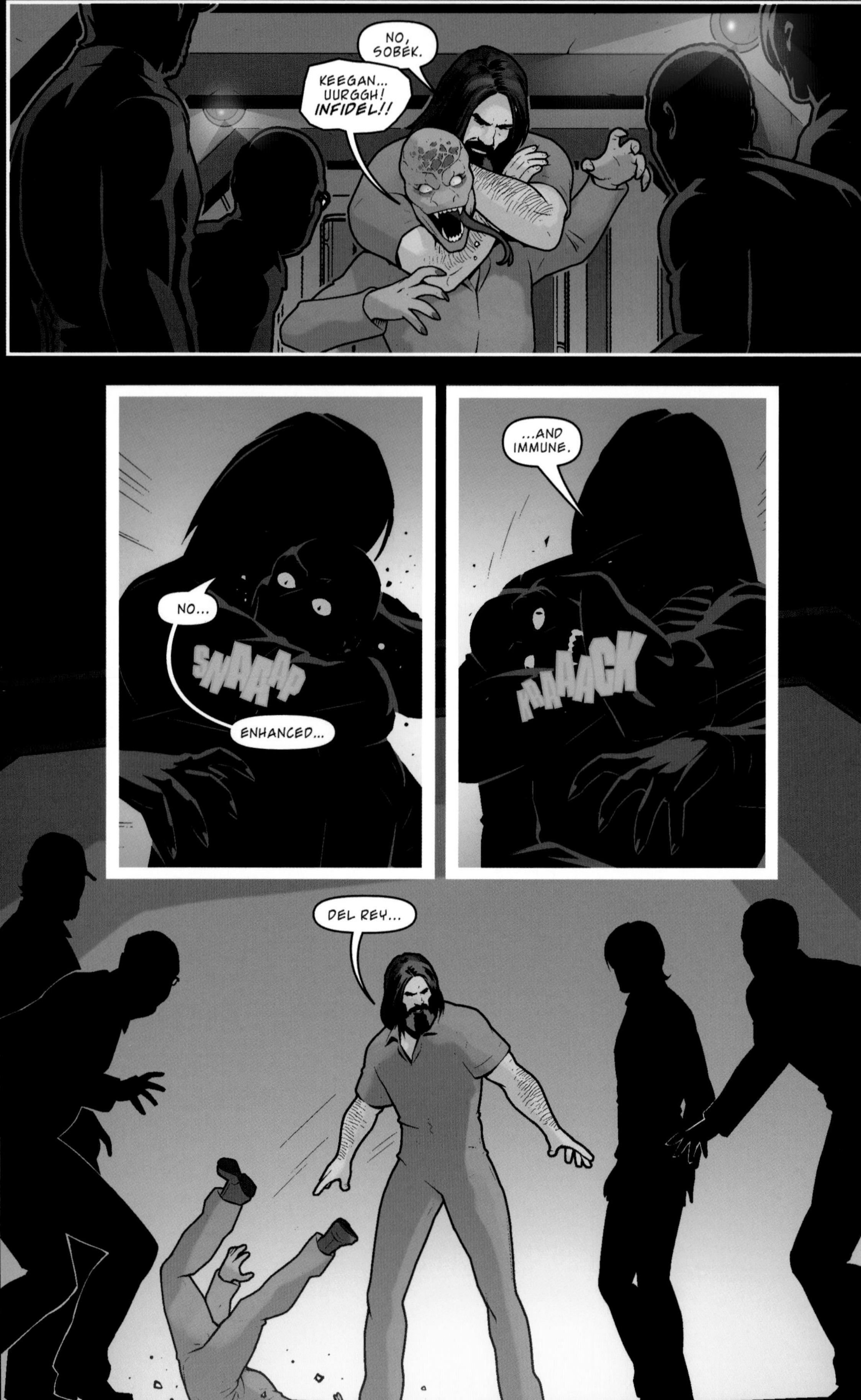
NO, SOBEK.
KEEGAN... UURGGH! INFIDEL!!
NO...
SNAAAP
ENHANCED...
...AND IMMUNE.
KRAAACK
DEL REY...

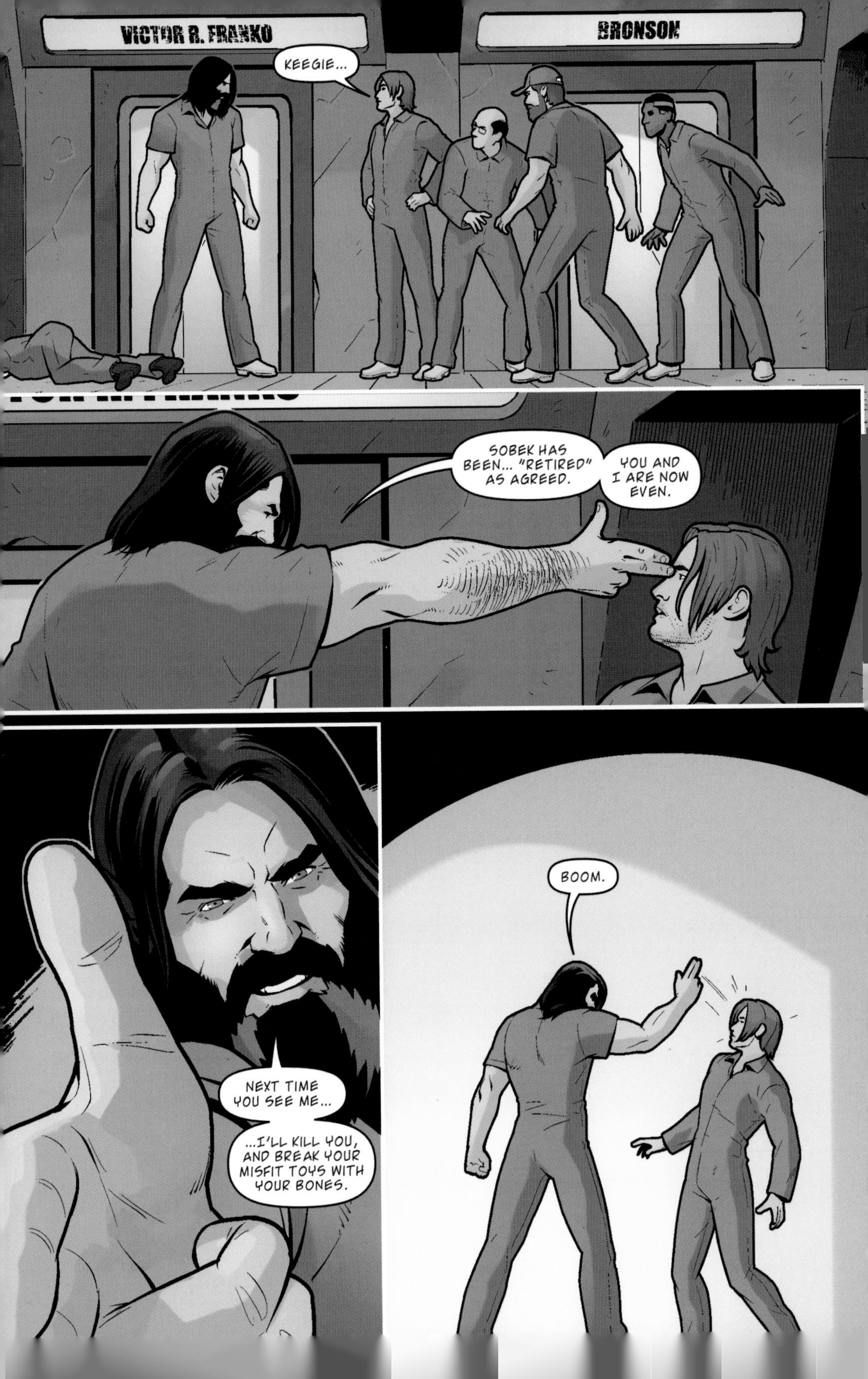

VICTOR R. FRANKO
BRONSON
KEEGIE...
SOBEK HAS BEEN... "RETIRED" AS AGREED.
YOU AND I ARE NOW EVEN.
NEXT TIME YOU SEE ME...
...I'LL KILL YOU, AND BREAK YOUR MISFIT TOYS WITH YOUR BONES.
BOOM.

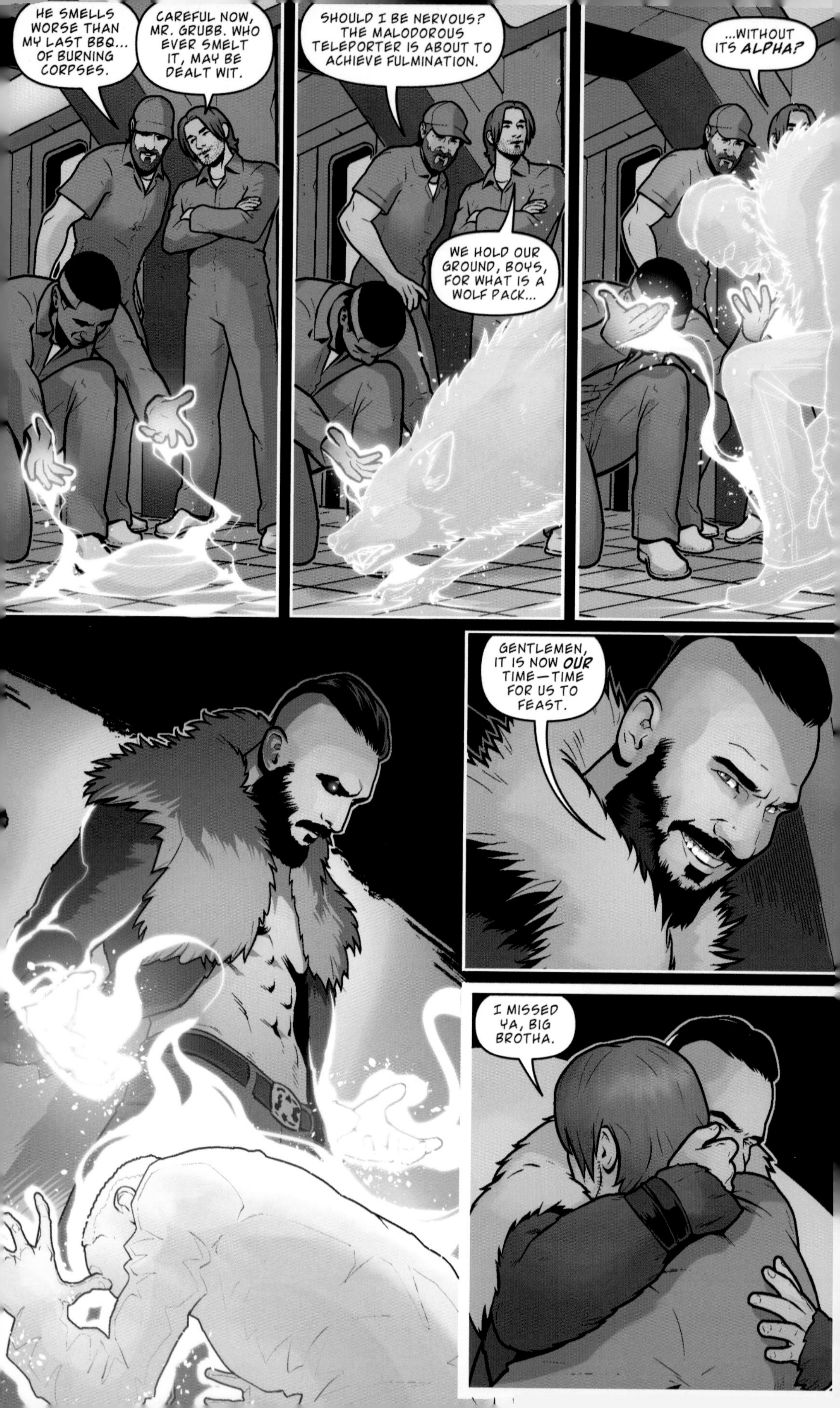
HE SMELLS WORSE THAN MY LAST BBQ... OF BURNING CORPSES.
CAREFUL NOW, MR. GRUBB. WHO EVER SMELT IT, MAY BE DEALT WIT.
SHOULD I BE NERVOUS? THE MALODOROUS TELEPORTER IS ABOUT TO ACHIEVE FULMINATION.
WE HOLD OUR GROUND, BOYS, FOR WHAT IS A WOLF PACK...
...WITHOUT ITS ALPHA?
GENTLEMEN, IT IS NOW OUR TIME—TIME FOR US TO FEAST.
I MISSED YA, BIG BROTHA.

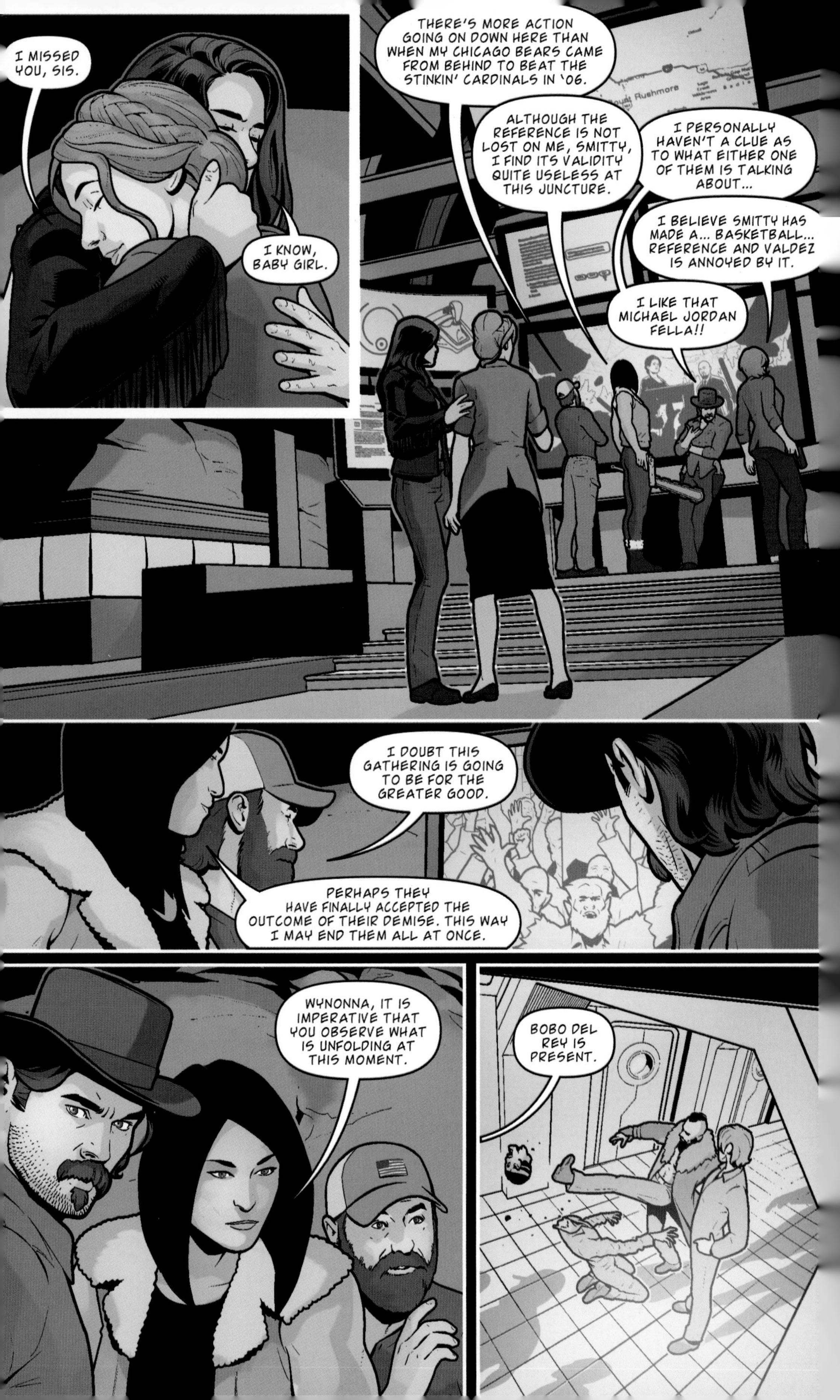
I MISSED YOU, SIS.
I KNOW, BABY GIRL.
THERE'S MORE ACTION GOING ON DOWN HERE THAN WHEN MY CHICAGO BEARS CAME FROM BEHIND TO BEAT THE STINKIN' CARDINALS IN '06.
ALTHOUGH THE REFERENCE IS NOT LOST ON ME, SMITTY, I FIND ITS VALIDITY QUITE USELESS AT THIS JUNCTURE.
I PERSONALLY HAVEN'T A CLUE AS TO WHAT EITHER ONE OF THEM IS TALKING ABOUT...
I BELIEVE SMITTY HAS MADE A... BASKETBALL... REFERENCE AND VALDEZ IS ANNOYED BY IT.
I LIKE THAT MICHAEL JORDAN FELLA!!
I DOUBT THIS GATHERING IS GOING TO BE FOR THE GREATER GOOD.
PERHAPS THEY HAVE FINALLY ACCEPTED THE OUTCOME OF THEIR DEMISE. THIS WAY I MAY END THEM ALL AT ONCE.
WYNONNA, IT IS IMPERATIVE THAT YOU OBSERVE WHAT IS UNFOLDING AT THIS MOMENT.
BOBO DEL REY IS PRESENT.

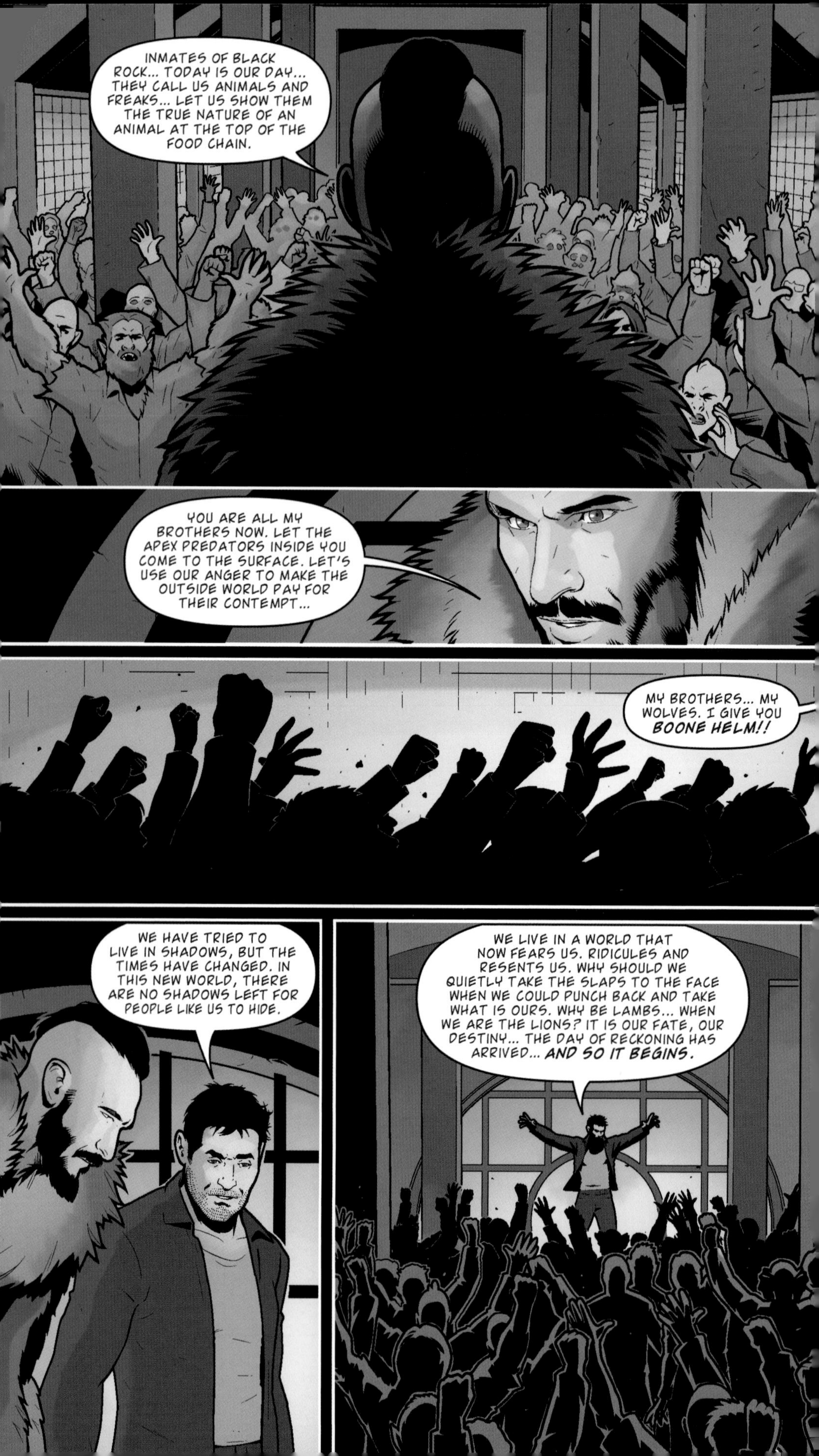
INMATES OF BLACK ROCK... TODAY IS OUR DAY... THEY CALL US ANIMALS AND FREAKS... LET US SHOW THEM THE TRUE NATURE OF AN ANIMAL AT THE TOP OF THE FOOD CHAIN.
YOU ARE ALL MY BROTHERS NOW. LET THE APEX PREDATORS INSIDE YOU COME TO THE SURFACE. LET'S USE OUR ANGER TO MAKE THE OUTSIDE WORLD PAY FOR THEIR CONTEMPT...
MY BROTHERS... MY WOLVES. I GIVE YOU ***BOONE HELM!!***
WE HAVE TRIED TO LIVE IN SHADOWS, BUT THE TIMES HAVE CHANGED. IN THIS NEW WORLD, THERE ARE NO SHADOWS LEFT FOR PEOPLE LIKE US TO HIDE.
WE LIVE IN A WORLD THAT NOW FEARS US. RIDICULES AND RESENTS US. WHY SHOULD WE QUIETLY TAKE THE SLAPS TO THE FACE WHEN WE COULD PUNCH BACK AND TAKE WHAT IS OURS. WHY BE LAMBS... WHEN WE ARE THE LIONS? IT IS OUR FATE, OUR DESTINY... THE DAY OF RECKONING HAS ARRIVED... ***AND SO IT BEGINS.***

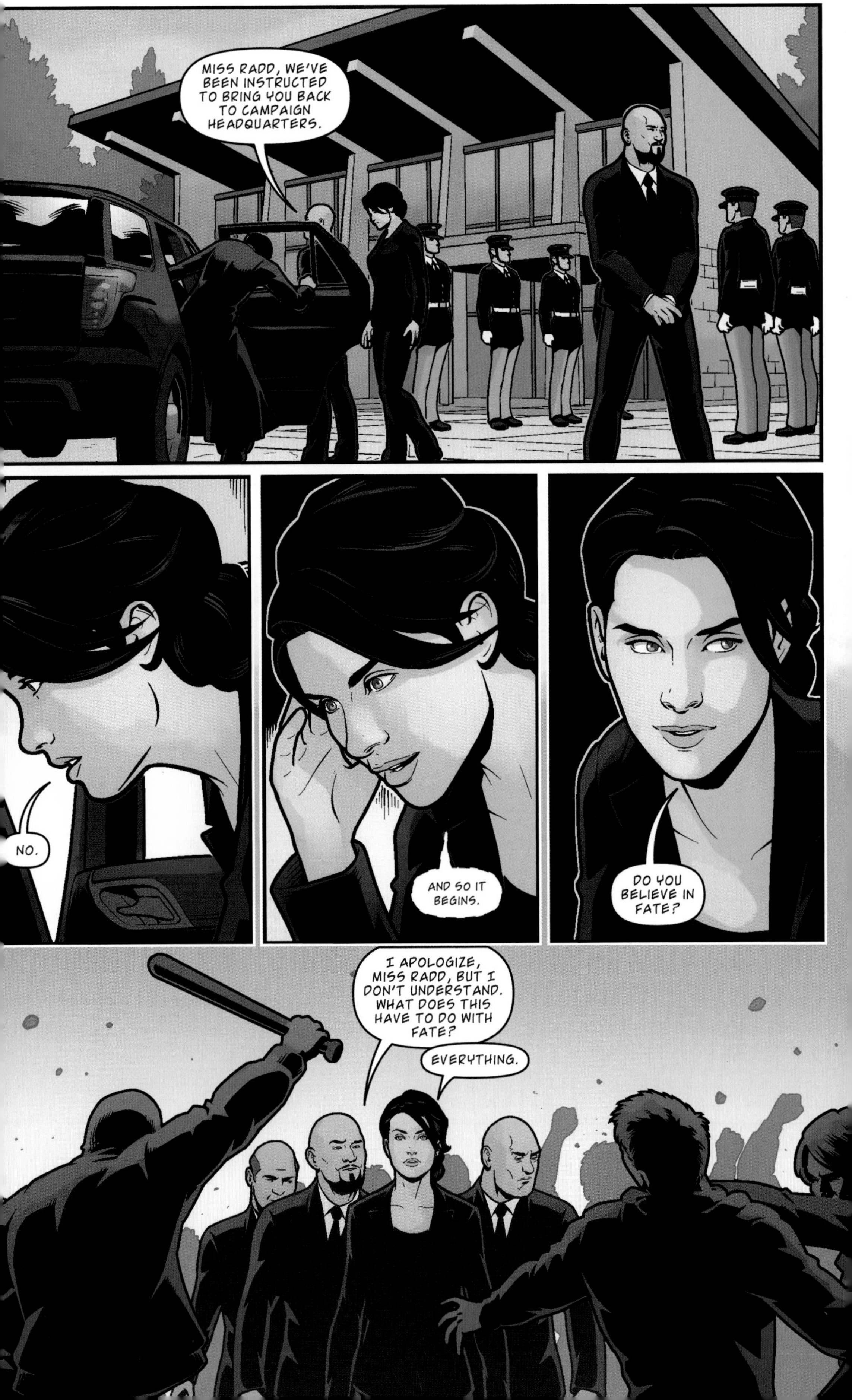
MISS RADD, WE'VE BEEN INSTRUCTED TO BRING YOU BACK TO CAMPAIGN HEADQUARTERS.
NO.
AND SO IT BEGINS.
DO YOU BELIEVE IN FATE?
I APOLOGIZE, MISS RADD, BUT I DON'T UNDERSTAND. WHAT DOES THIS HAVE TO DO WITH FATE?
EVERYTHING.

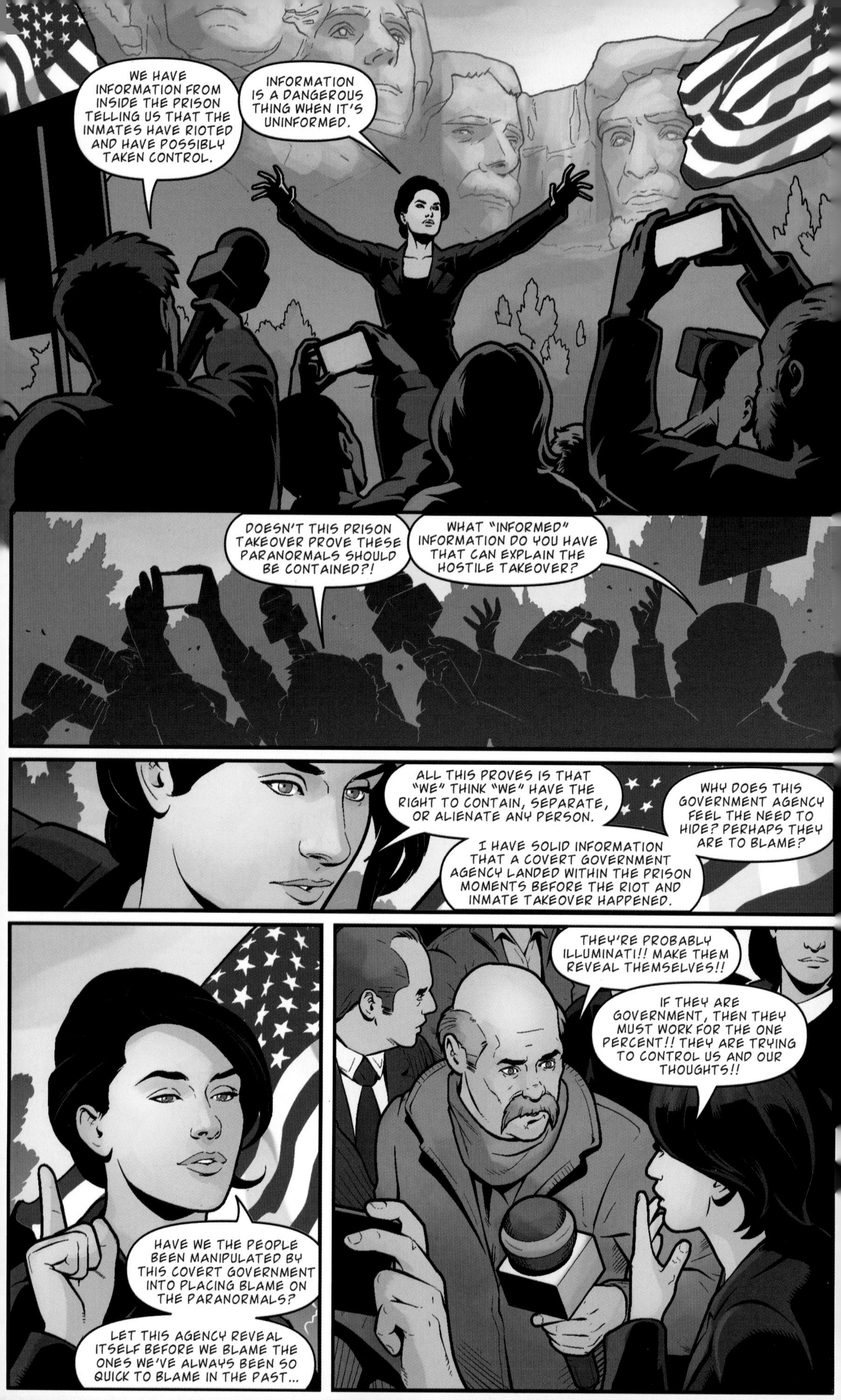
WE HAVE INFORMATION FROM INSIDE THE PRISON TELLING US THAT THE INMATES HAVE RIOTED AND HAVE POSSIBLY TAKEN CONTROL.
INFORMATION IS A DANGEROUS THING WHEN IT'S UNINFORMED.
DOESN'T THIS PRISON TAKEOVER PROVE THESE PARANORMALS SHOULD BE CONTAINED?!
WHAT "INFORMED" INFORMATION DO YOU HAVE THAT CAN EXPLAIN THE HOSTILE TAKEOVER?
ALL THIS PROVES IS THAT "WE" THINK "WE" HAVE THE RIGHT TO CONTAIN, SEPARATE, OR ALIENATE ANY PERSON.
I HAVE SOLID INFORMATION THAT A COVERT GOVERNMENT AGENCY LANDED WITHIN THE PRISON MOMENTS BEFORE THE RIOT AND INMATE TAKEOVER HAPPENED.
WHY DOES THIS GOVERNMENT AGENCY FEEL THE NEED TO HIDE? PERHAPS THEY ARE TO BLAME?
HAVE WE THE PEOPLE BEEN MANIPULATED BY THIS COVERT GOVERNMENT INTO PLACING BLAME ON THE PARANORMALS?
LET THIS AGENCY REVEAL ITSELF BEFORE WE BLAME THE ONES WE'VE ALWAYS BEEN SO QUICK TO BLAME IN THE PAST...
THEY'RE PROBABLY ILLUMINATI!! MAKE THEM REVEAL THEMSELVES!!
IF THEY ARE GOVERNMENT, THEN THEY MUST WORK FOR THE ONE PERCENT!! THEY ARE TRYING TO CONTROL US AND OUR THOUGHTS!!

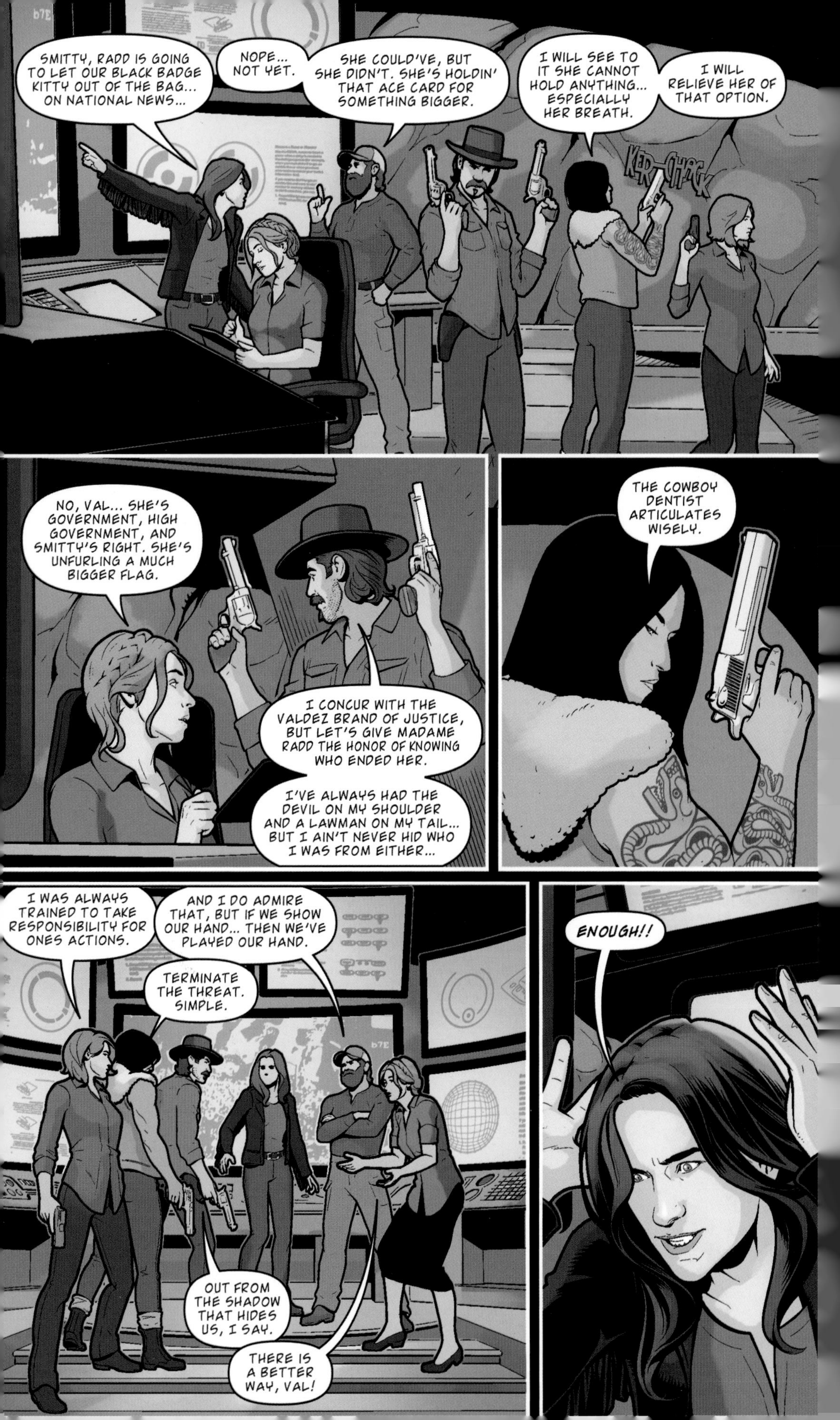
SMITTY, RADD IS GOING TO LET OUR BLACK BADGE KITTY OUT OF THE BAG... ON NATIONAL NEWS...
NOPE... NOT YET.
SHE COULD'VE, BUT SHE DIDN'T. SHE'S HOLDIN' THAT ACE CARD FOR SOMETHING BIGGER.
I WILL SEE TO IT SHE CANNOT HOLD ANYTHING... ESPECIALLY HER BREATH.
I WILL RELIEVE HER OF THAT OPTION.
KER-CHACK
NO, VAL... SHE'S GOVERNMENT, HIGH GOVERNMENT, AND SMITTY'S RIGHT. SHE'S UNFURLING A MUCH BIGGER FLAG.
I CONCUR WITH THE VALDEZ BRAND OF JUSTICE, BUT LET'S GIVE MADAME RADD THE HONOR OF KNOWING WHO ENDED HER.
I'VE ALWAYS HAD THE DEVIL ON MY SHOULDER AND A LAWMAN ON MY TAIL... BUT I AIN'T NEVER HID WHO I WAS FROM EITHER...
THE COWBOY DENTIST ARTICULATES WISELY.
I WAS ALWAYS TRAINED TO TAKE RESPONSIBILITY FOR ONES ACTIONS.
AND I DO ADMIRE THAT, BUT IF WE SHOW OUR HAND... THEN WE'VE PLAYED OUR HAND.
TERMINATE THE THREAT. SIMPLE.
OUT FROM THE SHADOW THAT HIDES US, I SAY.
THERE IS A BETTER WAY, VAL!
ENOUGH!!

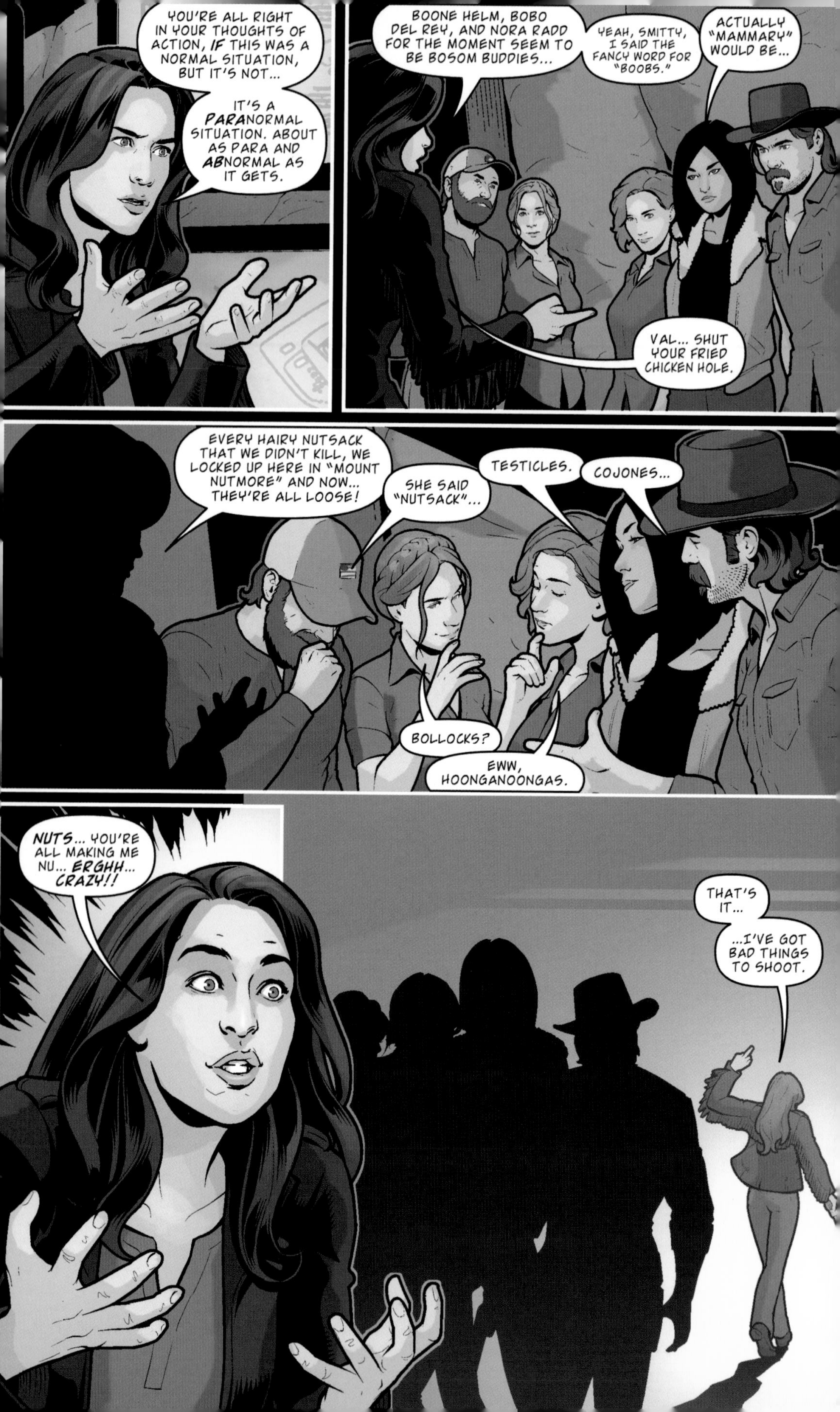
YOU'RE ALL RIGHT IN YOUR THOUGHTS OF ACTION, IF THIS WAS A NORMAL SITUATION, BUT IT'S NOT...
IT'S A PARANORMAL SITUATION. ABOUT AS PARA AND ABNORMAL AS IT GETS.
BOONE HELM, BOBO DEL REY, AND NORA RADD FOR THE MOMENT SEEM TO BE BOSOM BUDDIES...
YEAH, SMITTY, I SAID THE FANCY WORD FOR "BOOBS."
ACTUALLY "MAMMARY" WOULD BE...
VAL... SHUT YOUR FRIED CHICKEN HOLE.
EVERY HAIRY NUTSACK THAT WE DIDN'T KILL, WE LOCKED UP HERE IN "MOUNT NUTMORE" AND NOW... THEY'RE ALL LOOSE!
SHE SAID "NUTSACK"...
TESTICLES.
COJONES...
BOLLOCKS?
EWW, HOONGANOONGAS.
NUTS... YOU'RE ALL MAKING ME NU... ERGHH... CRAZY!!
THAT'S IT...
...I'VE GOT BAD THINGS TO SHOOT.

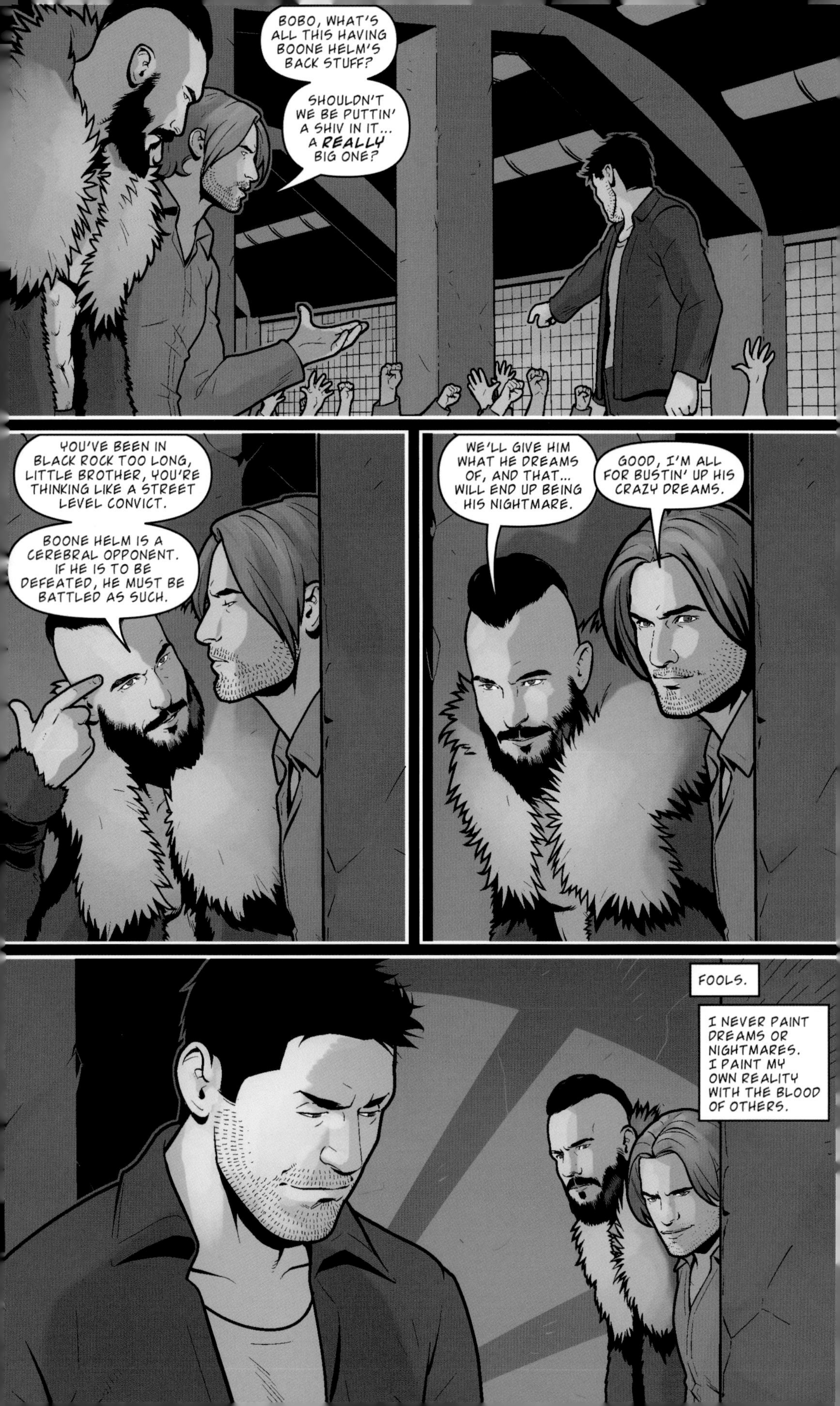
BOBO, WHAT'S ALL THIS HAVING BOONE HELM'S BACK STUFF?
SHOULDN'T WE BE PUTTIN' A SHIV IN IT... A REALLY BIG ONE?
YOU'VE BEEN IN BLACK ROCK TOO LONG, LITTLE BROTHER, YOU'RE THINKING LIKE A STREET LEVEL CONVICT.
BOONE HELM IS A CEREBRAL OPPONENT. IF HE IS TO BE DEFEATED, HE MUST BE BATTLED AS SUCH.
WE'LL GIVE HIM WHAT HE DREAMS OF, AND THAT... WILL END UP BEING HIS NIGHTMARE.
GOOD, I'M ALL FOR BUSTIN' UP HIS CRAZY DREAMS.
FOOLS.
I NEVER PAINT DREAMS OR NIGHTMARES. I PAINT MY OWN REALITY WITH THE BLOOD OF OTHERS.

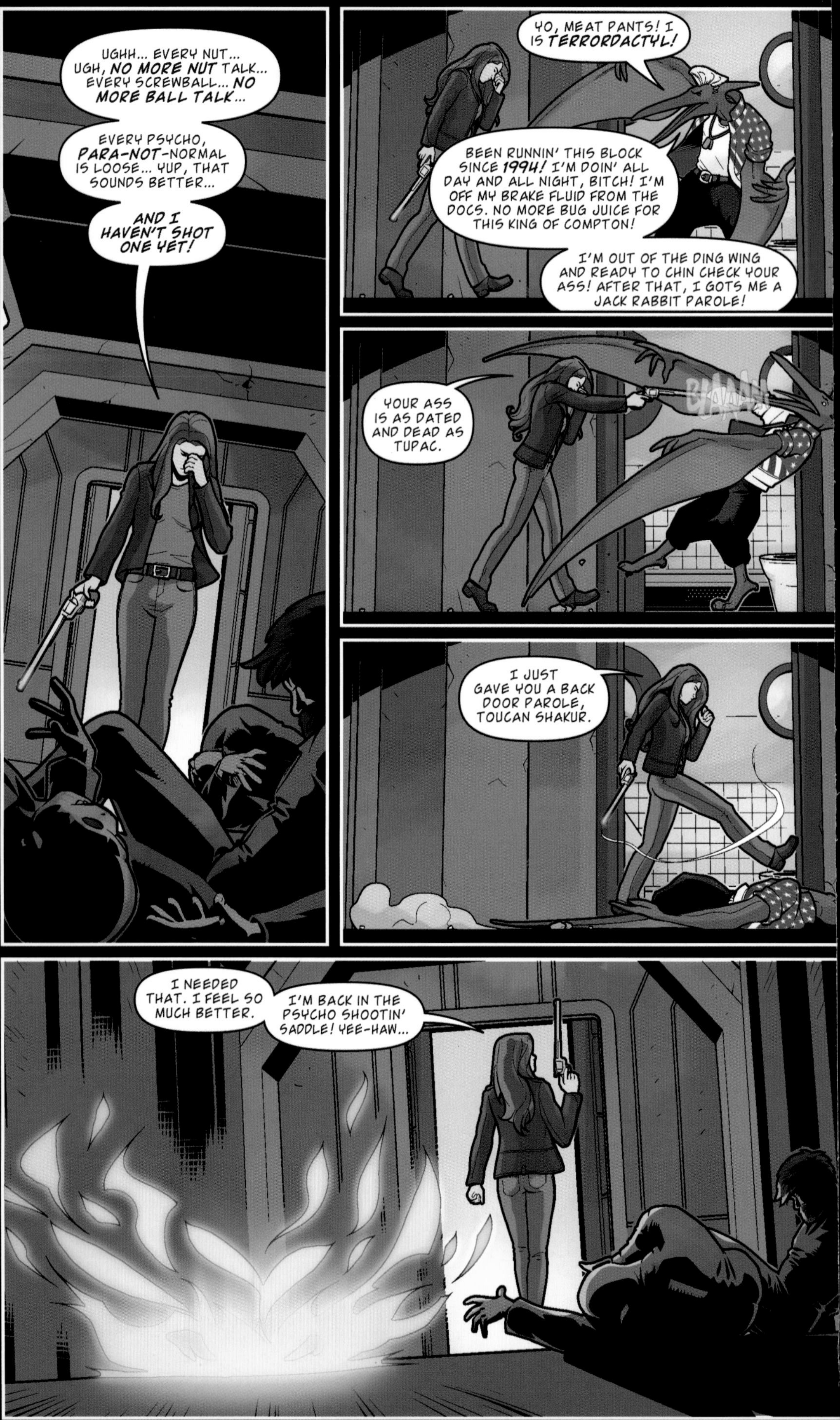
UGHH... EVERY NUT... UGH, NO MORE NUT TALK... EVERY SCREWBALL... NO MORE BALL TALK...
EVERY PSYCHO, PARA-NOT-NORMAL IS LOOSE... YUP, THAT SOUNDS BETTER...
AND I HAVEN'T SHOT ONE YET!
YO, MEAT PANTS! I IS TERRORDACTYL!
BEEN RUNNIN' THIS BLOCK SINCE 1994! I'M DOIN' ALL DAY AND ALL NIGHT, BITCH! I'M OFF MY BRAKE FLUID FROM THE DOCS. NO MORE BUG JUICE FOR THIS KING OF COMPTON!
I'M OUT OF THE DING WING AND READY TO CHIN CHECK YOUR ASS! AFTER THAT, I GOTS ME A JACK RABBIT PAROLE!
YOUR ASS IS AS DATED AND DEAD AS TUPAC.
BLAAAM
I JUST GAVE YOU A BACK DOOR PAROLE, TOUCAN SHAKUR.
I NEEDED THAT. I FEEL SO MUCH BETTER.
I'M BACK IN THE PSYCHO SHOOTIN' SADDLE! YEE-HAW...

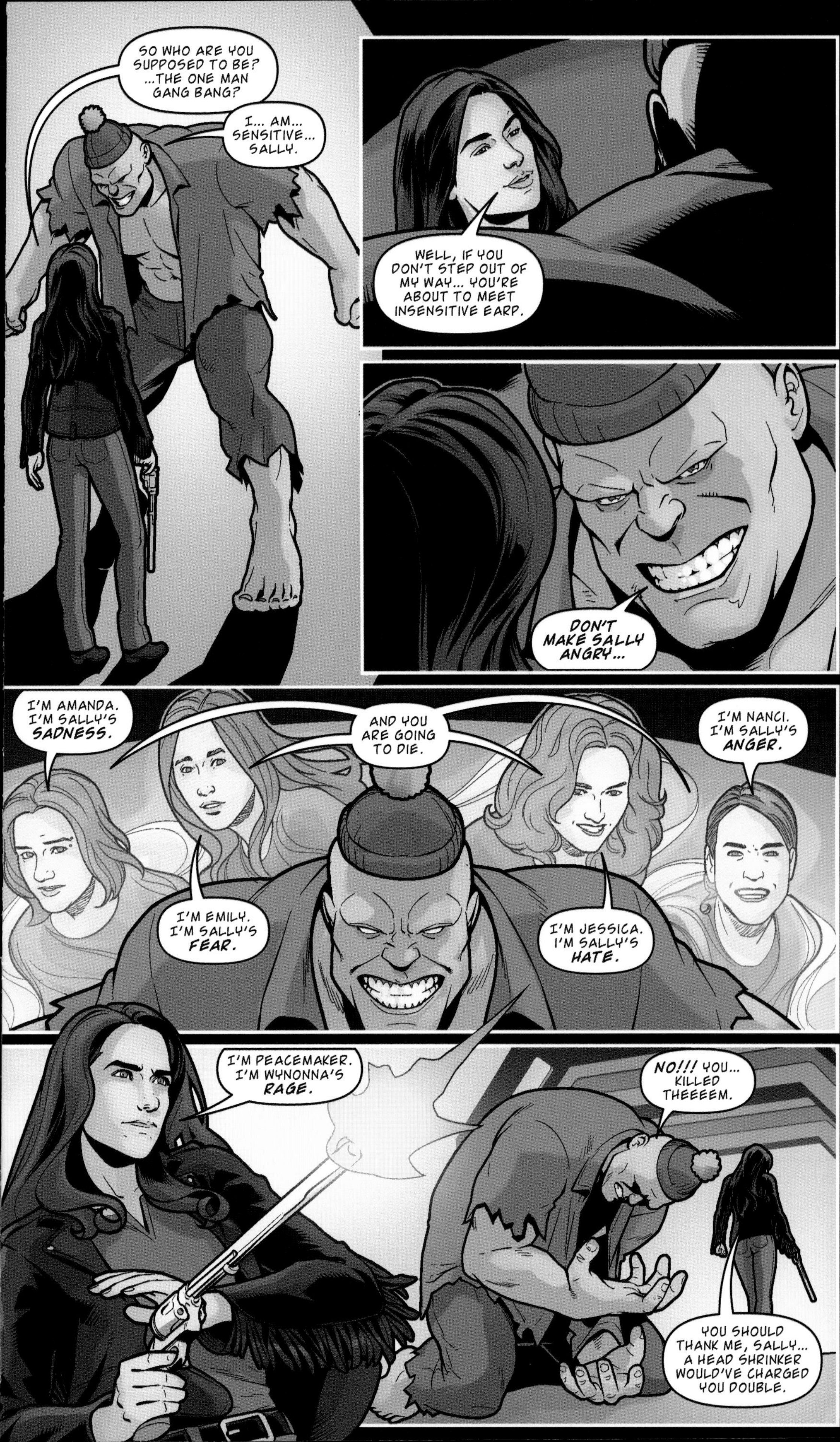
SO WHO ARE YOU SUPPOSED TO BE? ...THE ONE MAN GANG BANG?
I... AM... SENSITIVE... SALLY.
WELL, IF YOU DON'T STEP OUT OF MY WAY... YOU'RE ABOUT TO MEET INSENSITIVE EARP.
DON'T MAKE SALLY ANGRY...
I'M AMANDA. I'M SALLY'S SADNESS.
AND YOU ARE GOING TO DIE.
I'M NANCI. I'M SALLY'S ANGER.
I'M EMILY. I'M SALLY'S FEAR.
I'M JESSICA. I'M SALLY'S HATE.
I'M PEACEMAKER. I'M WYNONNA'S RAGE.
NO!!! YOU... KILLED THEEEEM.
YOU SHOULD THANK ME, SALLY... A HEAD SHRINKER WOULD'VE CHARGED YOU DOUBLE.

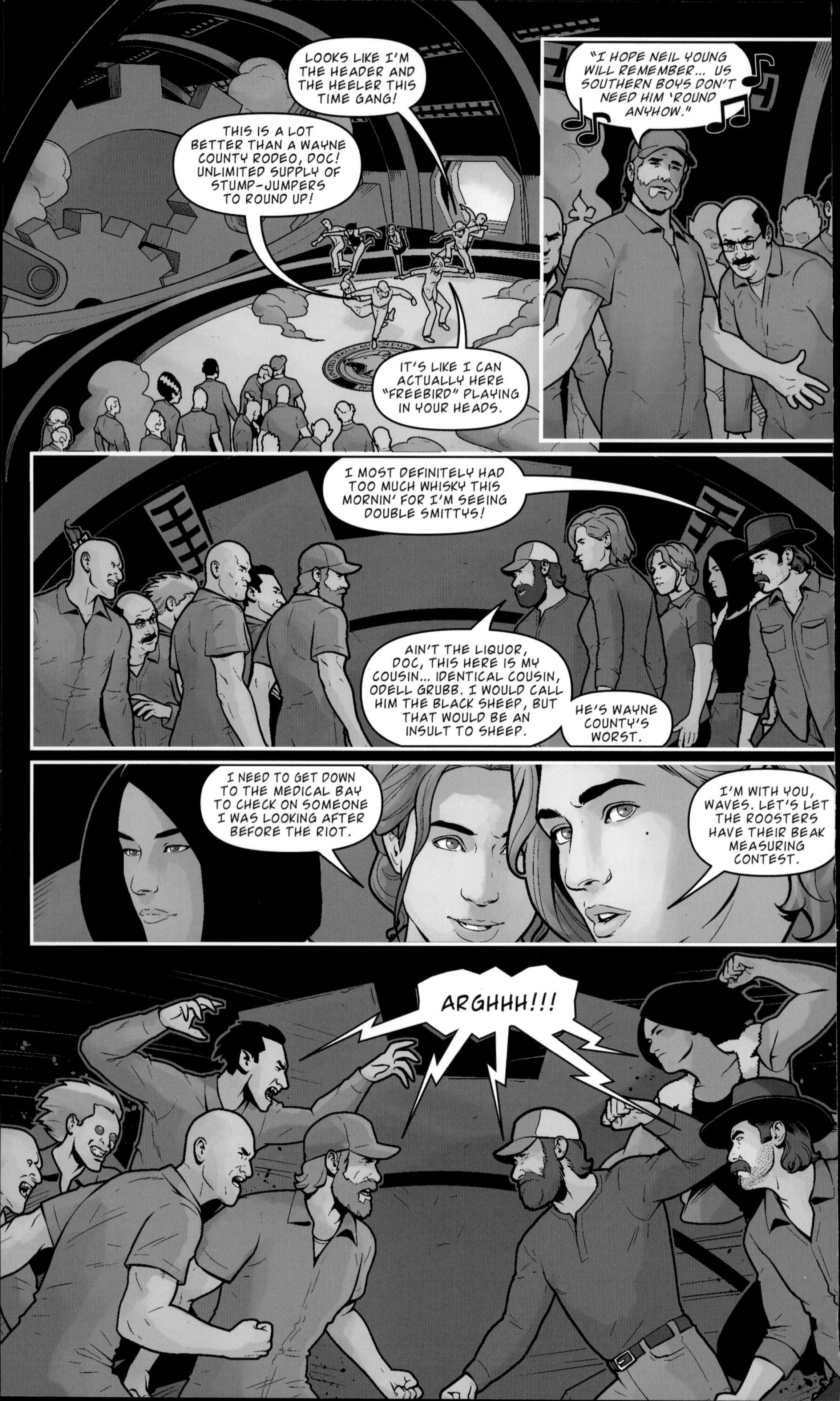
LOOKS LIKE I'M THE HEADER AND THE HEELER THIS TIME GANG!
THIS IS A LOT BETTER THAN A WAYNE COUNTY RODEO, DOC! UNLIMITED SUPPLY OF STUMP-JUMPERS TO ROUND UP!
IT'S LIKE I CAN ACTUALLY HERE "FREEBIRD" PLAYING IN YOUR HEADS.
"I HOPE NEIL YOUNG WILL REMEMBER... US SOUTHERN BOYS DON'T NEED HIM 'ROUND ANYHOW."
I MOST DEFINITELY HAD TOO MUCH WHISKY THIS MORNIN' FOR I'M SEEING DOUBLE SMITTYS!
AIN'T THE LIQUOR, DOC, THIS HERE IS MY COUSIN... IDENTICAL COUSIN, ODELL GRUBB. I WOULD CALL HIM THE BLACK SHEEP, BUT THAT WOULD BE AN INSULT TO SHEEP.
HE'S WAYNE COUNTY'S WORST.
I NEED TO GET DOWN TO THE MEDICAL BAY TO CHECK ON SOMEONE I WAS LOOKING AFTER BEFORE THE RIOT.
I'M WITH YOU, WAVES. LET'S LET THE ROOSTERS HAVE THEIR BEAK MEASURING CONTEST.
ARGHHH!!!

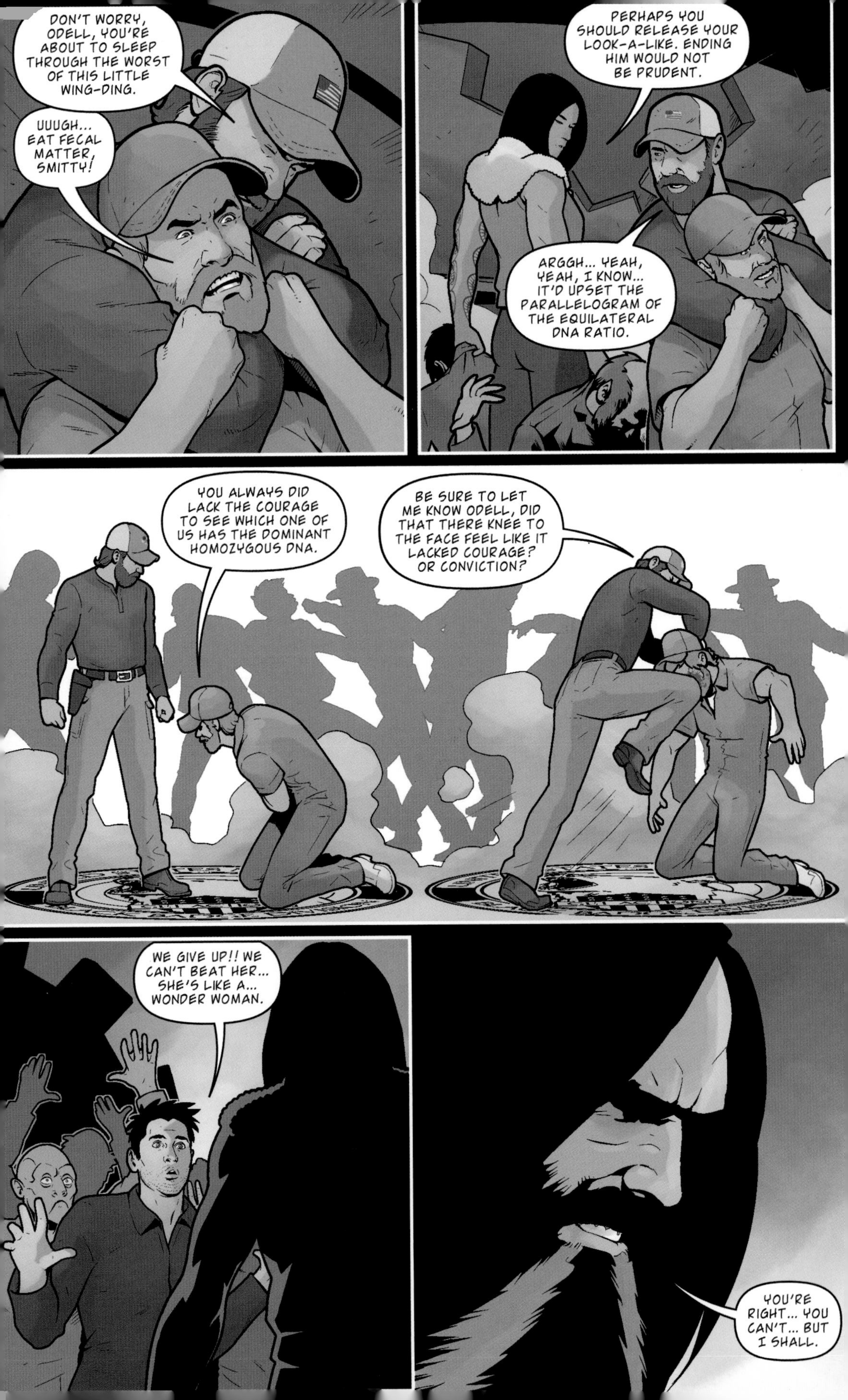
DON'T WORRY, ODELL, YOU'RE ABOUT TO SLEEP THROUGH THE WORST OF THIS LITTLE WING-DING.
UUUGH... EAT FECAL MATTER, SMITTY!
PERHAPS YOU SHOULD RELEASE YOUR LOOK-A-LIKE. ENDING HIM WOULD NOT BE PRUDENT.
ARGGH... YEAH, YEAH, I KNOW... IT'D UPSET THE PARALLELOGRAM OF THE EQUILATERAL DNA RATIO.
YOU ALWAYS DID LACK THE COURAGE TO SEE WHICH ONE OF US HAS THE DOMINANT HOMOZYGOUS DNA.
BE SURE TO LET ME KNOW ODELL, DID THAT THERE KNEE TO THE FACE FEEL LIKE IT LACKED COURAGE? OR CONVICTION?
WE GIVE UP!! WE CAN'T BEAT HER... SHE'S LIKE A... WONDER WOMAN.
YOU'RE RIGHT... YOU CAN'T... BUT I SHALL.

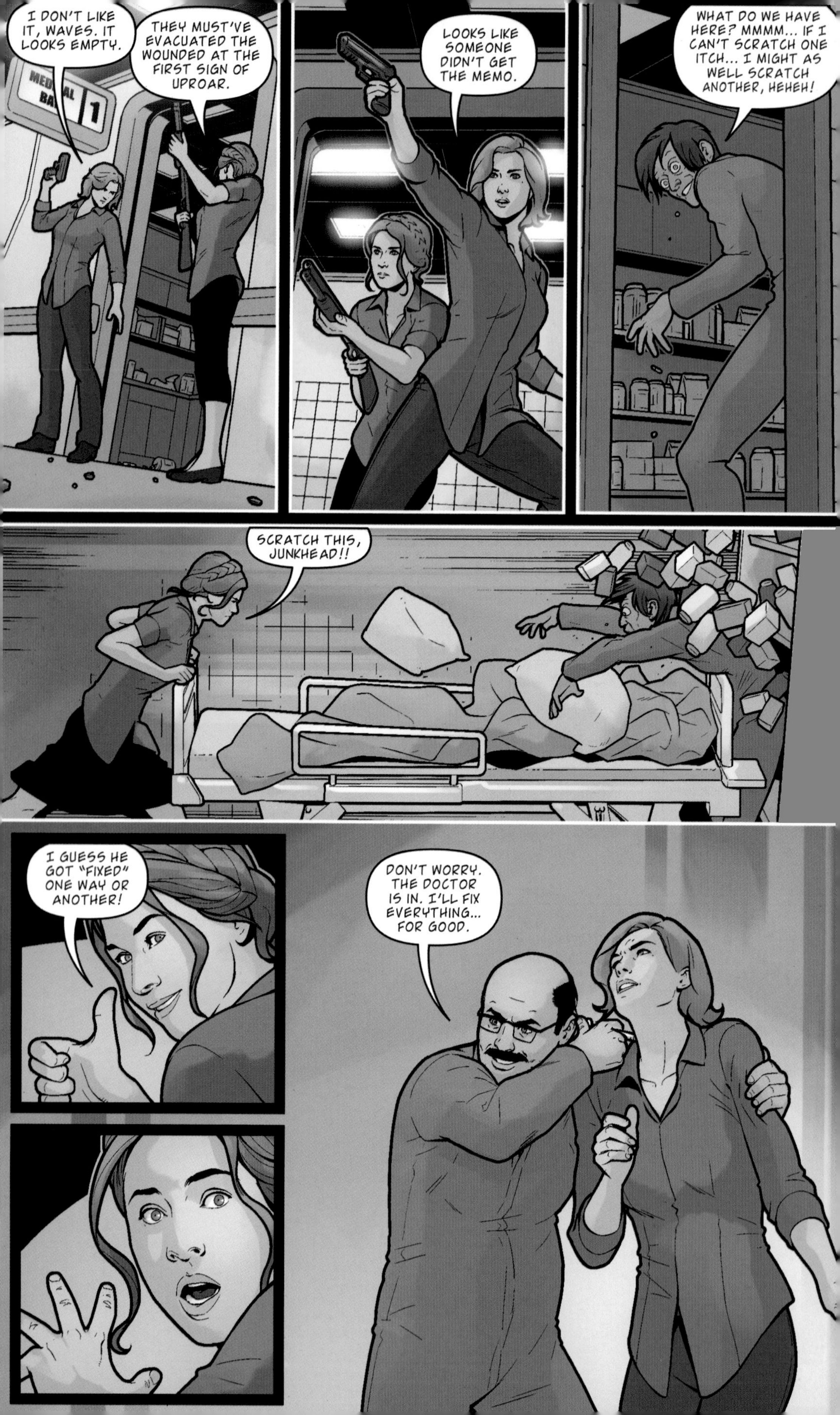
I DON'T LIKE IT, WAVES. IT LOOKS EMPTY.
THEY MUST'VE EVACUATED THE WOUNDED AT THE FIRST SIGN OF UPROAR.
LOOKS LIKE SOMEONE DIDN'T GET THE MEMO.
WHAT DO WE HAVE HERE? MMMM... IF I CAN'T SCRATCH ONE ITCH... I MIGHT AS WELL SCRATCH ANOTHER, HEHEH!
SCRATCH THIS, JUNKHEAD!!
I GUESS HE GOT "FIXED" ONE WAY OR ANOTHER!
DON'T WORRY. THE DOCTOR IS IN. I'LL FIX EVERYTHING... FOR GOOD.

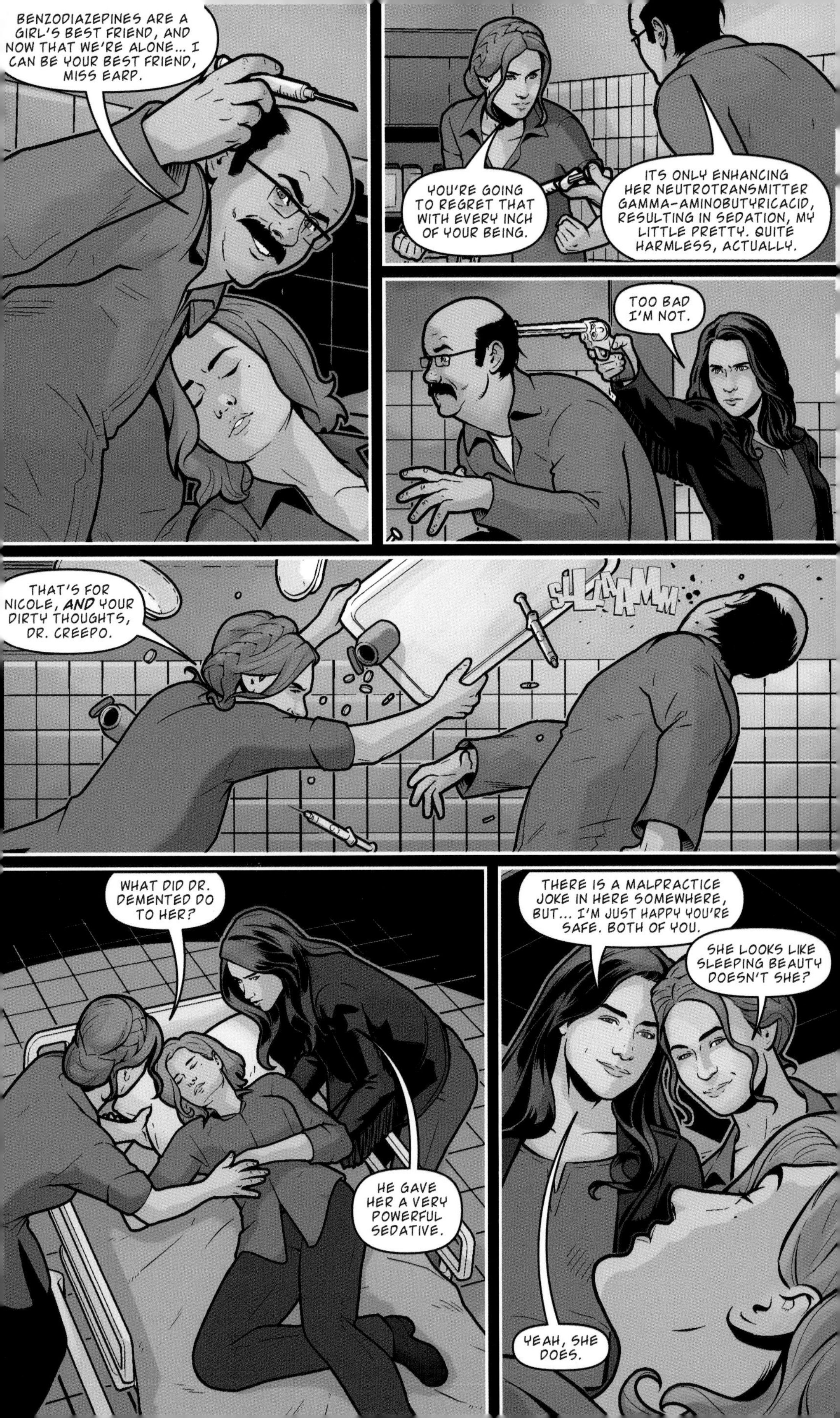
BENZODIAZEPINES ARE A GIRL'S BEST FRIEND, AND NOW THAT WE'RE ALONE... I CAN BE YOUR BEST FRIEND, MISS EARP.
YOU'RE GOING TO REGRET THAT WITH EVERY INCH OF YOUR BEING.
ITS ONLY ENHANCING HER NEUTROTRANSMITTER GAMMA-AMINOBUTYRICACID, RESULTING IN SEDATION, MY LITTLE PRETTY. QUITE HARMLESS, ACTUALLY.
TOO BAD I'M NOT.
THAT'S FOR NICOLE, AND YOUR DIRTY THOUGHTS, DR. CREEPO.
SLLAAMM
WHAT DID DR. DEMENTED DO TO HER?
HE GAVE HER A VERY POWERFUL SEDATIVE.
THERE IS A MALPRACTICE JOKE IN HERE SOMEWHERE, BUT... I'M JUST HAPPY YOU'RE SAFE. BOTH OF YOU.
SHE LOOKS LIKE SLEEPING BEAUTY DOESN'T SHE?
YEAH, SHE DOES.

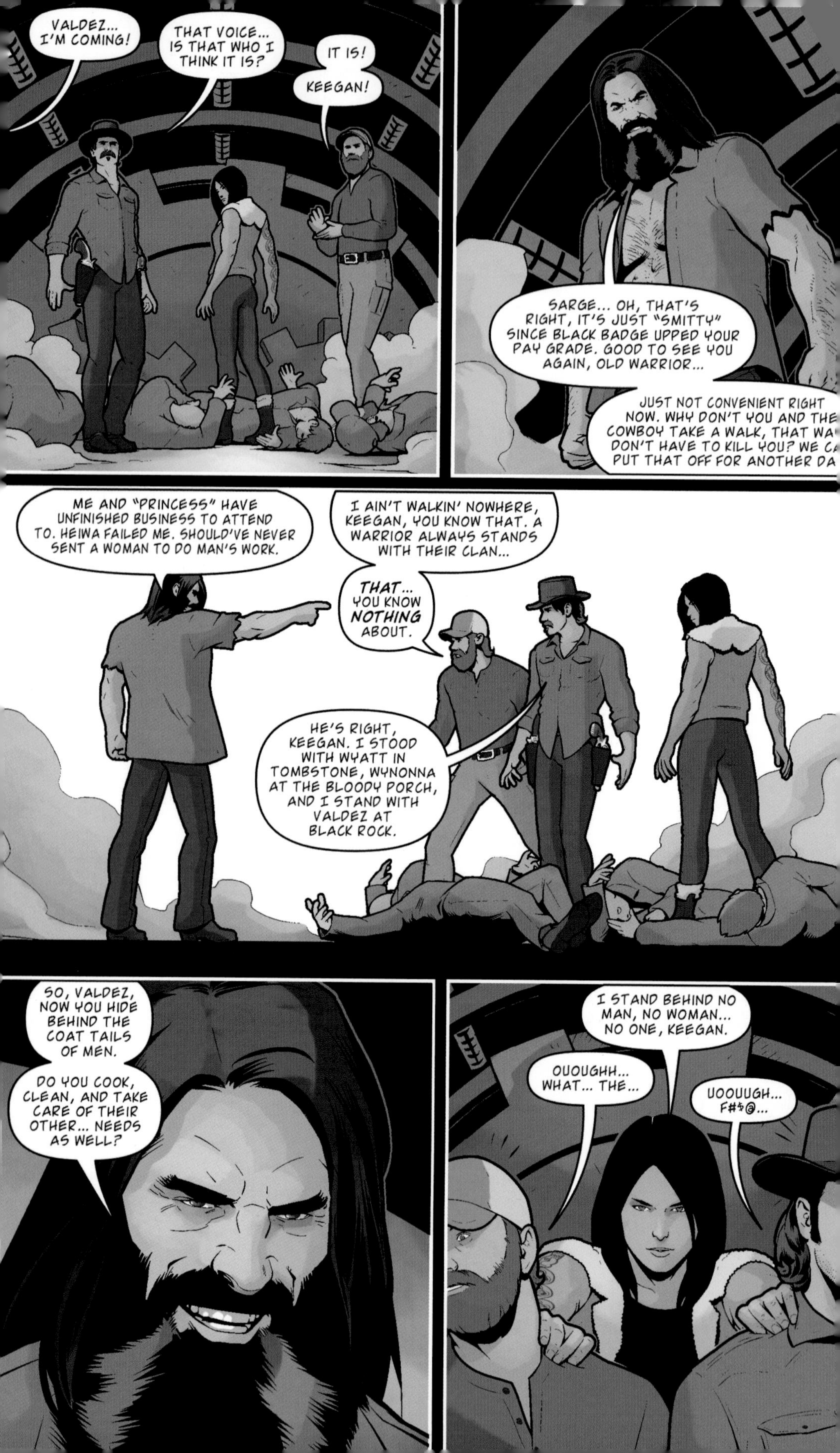

VALDEZ... I'M COMING!
THAT VOICE... IS THAT WHO I THINK IT IS?
IT IS!
KEEGAN!
SARGE... OH, THAT'S RIGHT, IT'S JUST "SMITTY" SINCE BLACK BADGE UPPED YOUR PAY GRADE. GOOD TO SEE YOU AGAIN, OLD WARRIOR...
JUST NOT CONVENIENT RIGHT NOW. WHY DON'T YOU AND THE COWBOY TAKE A WALK, THAT WA DON'T HAVE TO KILL YOU? WE CA PUT THAT OFF FOR ANOTHER DA
ME AND "PRINCESS" HAVE UNFINISHED BUSINESS TO ATTEND TO. HEIWA FAILED ME. SHOULD'VE NEVER SENT A WOMAN TO DO MAN'S WORK.
I AIN'T WALKIN' NOWHERE, KEEGAN, YOU KNOW THAT. A WARRIOR ALWAYS STANDS WITH THEIR CLAN...
THAT... YOU KNOW ***NOTHING*** ABOUT.
HE'S RIGHT, KEEGAN. I STOOD WITH WYATT IN TOMBSTONE, WYNONNA AT THE BLOODY PORCH, AND I STAND WITH VALDEZ AT BLACK ROCK.
SO, VALDEZ, NOW YOU HIDE BEHIND THE COAT TAILS OF MEN.
DO YOU COOK, CLEAN, AND TAKE CARE OF THEIR OTHER... NEEDS AS WELL?
I STAND BEHIND NO MAN, NO WOMAN... NO ONE, KEEGAN.
OUOUGHH... WHAT... THE...
UOOUUGH... F#$@...

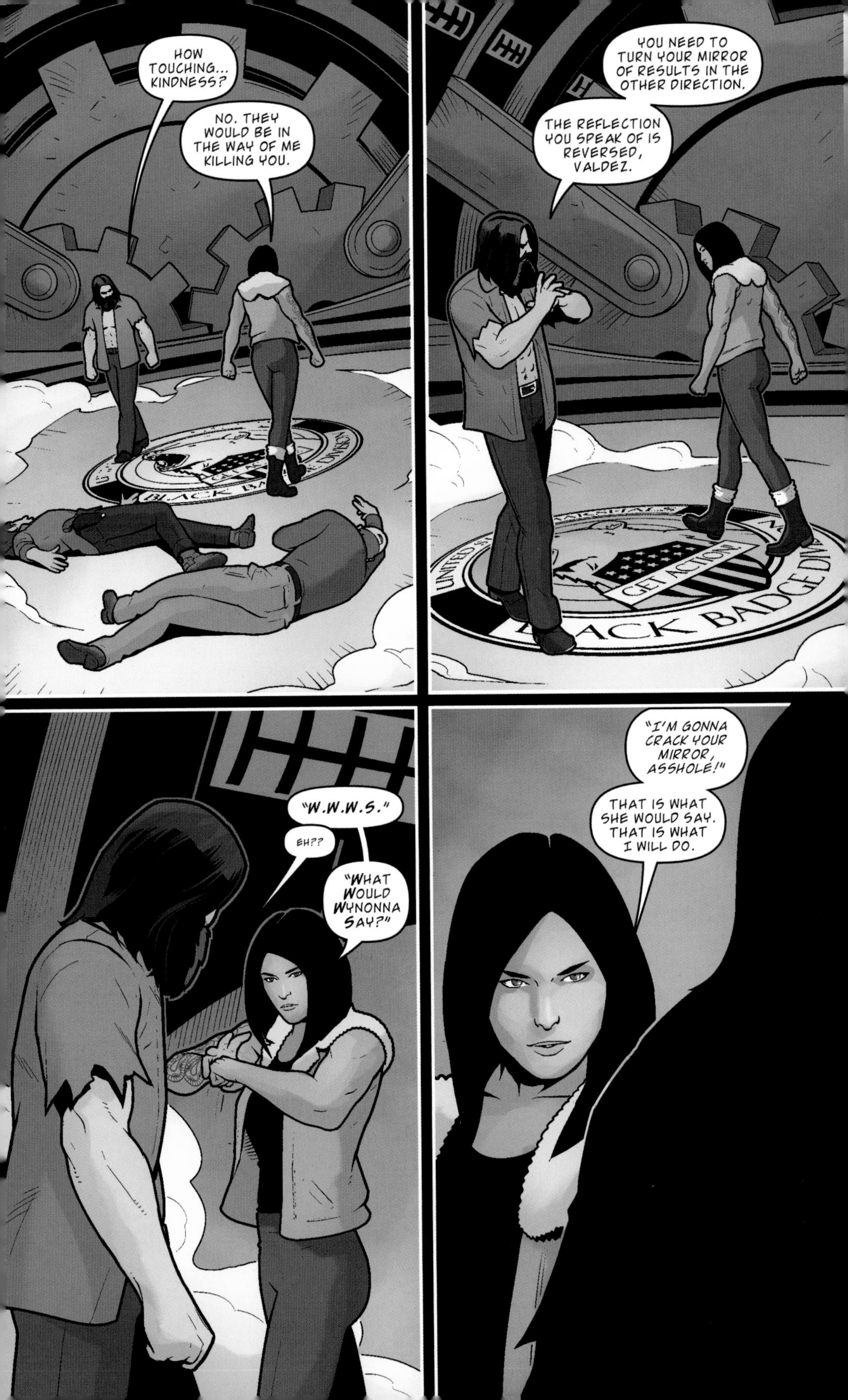
HOW TOUCHING... KINDNESS?
NO. THEY WOULD BE IN THE WAY OF ME KILLING YOU.
YOU NEED TO TURN YOUR MIRROR OF RESULTS IN THE OTHER DIRECTION.
THE REFLECTION YOU SPEAK OF IS REVERSED, VALDEZ.
GET ACTION!
BLACK BADGE DIV
"W.W.W.S."
EH??
"WHAT WOULD WYNONNA SAY?"
"I'M GONNA CRACK YOUR MIRROR, ASSHOLE!"
THAT IS WHAT SHE WOULD SAY. THAT IS WHAT I WILL DO.

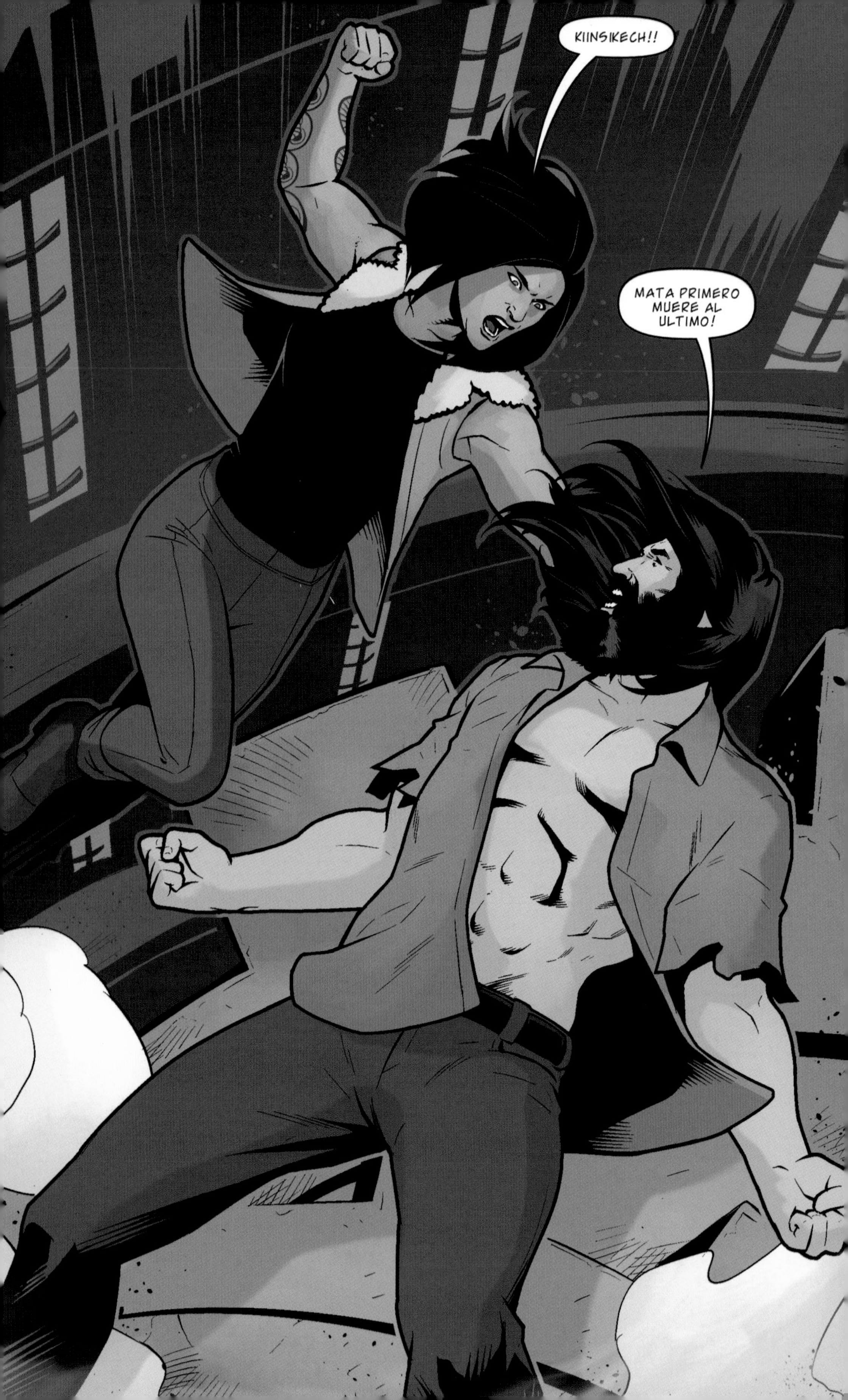
KIINSIKECH!!
MATA PRIMERO
MUERE AL
ULTIMO!

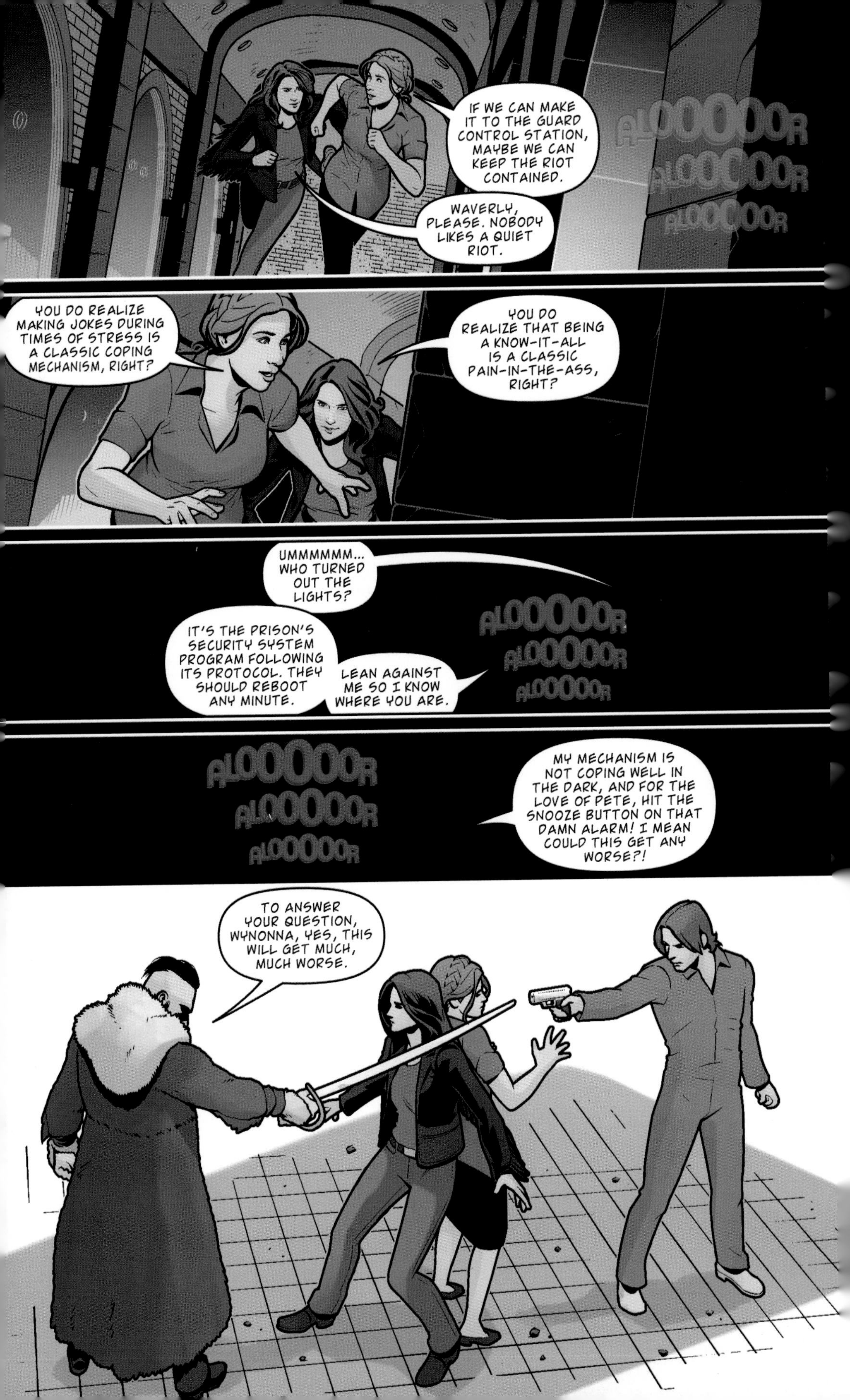
IF WE CAN MAKE IT TO THE GUARD CONTROL STATION, MAYBE WE CAN KEEP THE RIOT CONTAINED.
ALOOOOOR ALOOOOOR ALOOOOOR
WAVERLY, PLEASE. NOBODY LIKES A QUIET RIOT.
YOU DO REALIZE MAKING JOKES DURING TIMES OF STRESS IS A CLASSIC COPING MECHANISM, RIGHT?
YOU DO REALIZE THAT BEING A KNOW-IT-ALL IS A CLASSIC PAIN-IN-THE-ASS, RIGHT?
UMMMMMM... WHO TURNED OUT THE LIGHTS?
IT'S THE PRISON'S SECURITY SYSTEM PROGRAM FOLLOWING ITS PROTOCOL. THEY SHOULD REBOOT ANY MINUTE.
LEAN AGAINST ME SO I KNOW WHERE YOU ARE.
ALOOOOOR ALOOOOOR ALOOOOOR
ALOOOOOR ALOOOOOR ALOOOOOR
MY MECHANISM IS NOT COPING WELL IN THE DARK, AND FOR THE LOVE OF PETE, HIT THE SNOOZE BUTTON ON THAT DAMN ALARM! I MEAN COULD THIS GET ANY WORSE?!
TO ANSWER YOUR QUESTION, WYNONNA, YES, THIS WILL GET MUCH, MUCH WORSE.

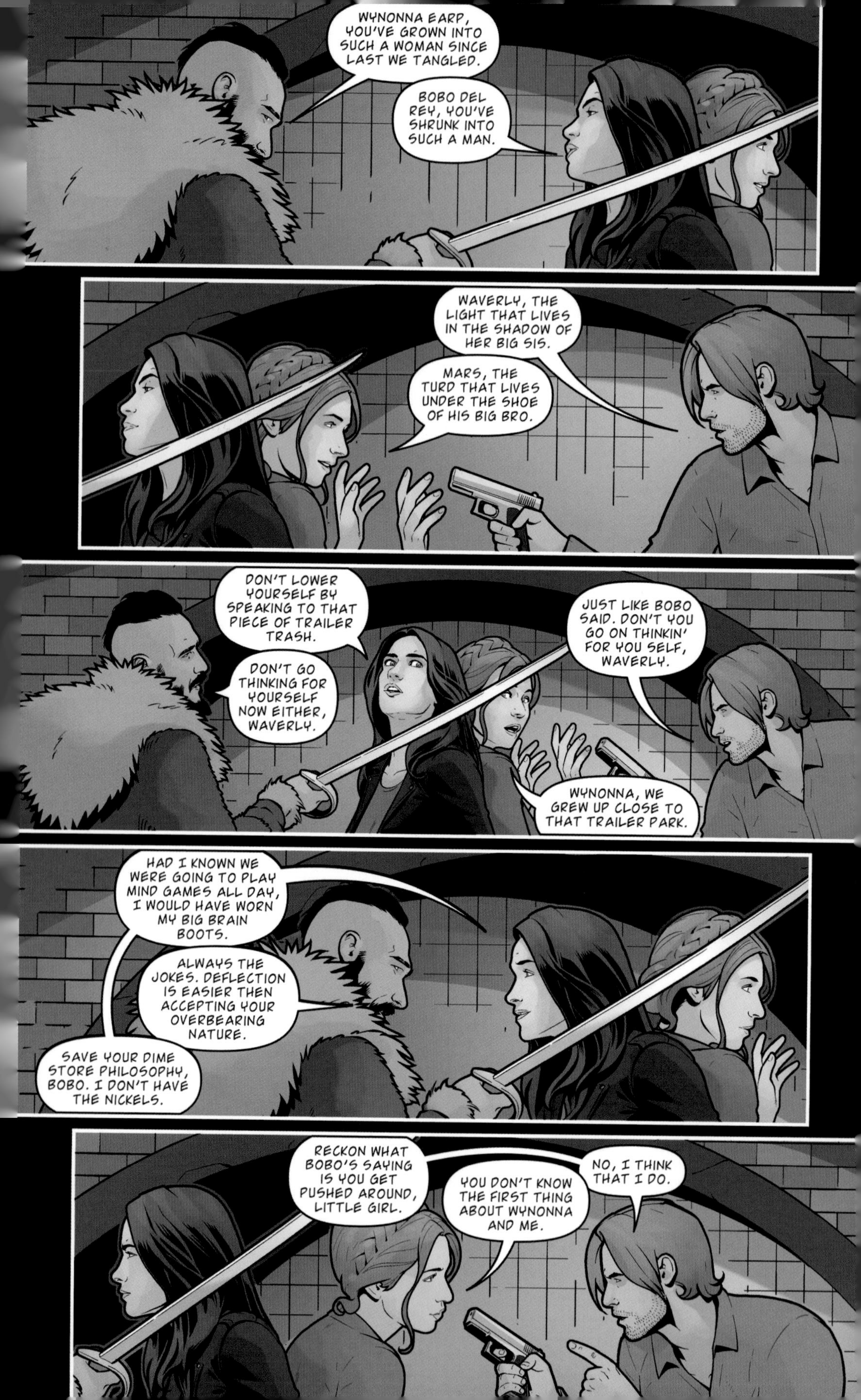
WYNONNA EARP, YOU'VE GROWN INTO SUCH A WOMAN SINCE LAST WE TANGLED.
BOBO DEL REY, YOU'VE SHRUNK INTO SUCH A MAN.
WAVERLY, THE LIGHT THAT LIVES IN THE SHADOW OF HER BIG SIS.
MARS, THE TURD THAT LIVES UNDER THE SHOE OF HIS BIG BRO.
DON'T LOWER YOURSELF BY SPEAKING TO THAT PIECE OF TRAILER TRASH.
DON'T GO THINKING FOR YOURSELF NOW EITHER, WAVERLY.
JUST LIKE BOBO SAID. DON'T YOU GO ON THINKIN' FOR YOU SELF, WAVERLY.
WYNONNA, WE GREW UP CLOSE TO THAT TRAILER PARK.
HAD I KNOWN WE WERE GOING TO PLAY MIND GAMES ALL DAY, I WOULD HAVE WORN MY BIG BRAIN BOOTS.
ALWAYS THE JOKES. DEFLECTION IS EASIER THEN ACCEPTING YOUR OVERBEARING NATURE.
SAVE YOUR DIME STORE PHILOSOPHY, BOBO. I DON'T HAVE THE NICKELS.
RECKON WHAT BOBO'S SAYING IS YOU GET PUSHED AROUND, LITTLE GIRL.
YOU DON'T KNOW THE FIRST THING ABOUT WYNONNA AND ME.
NO, I THINK THAT I DO.

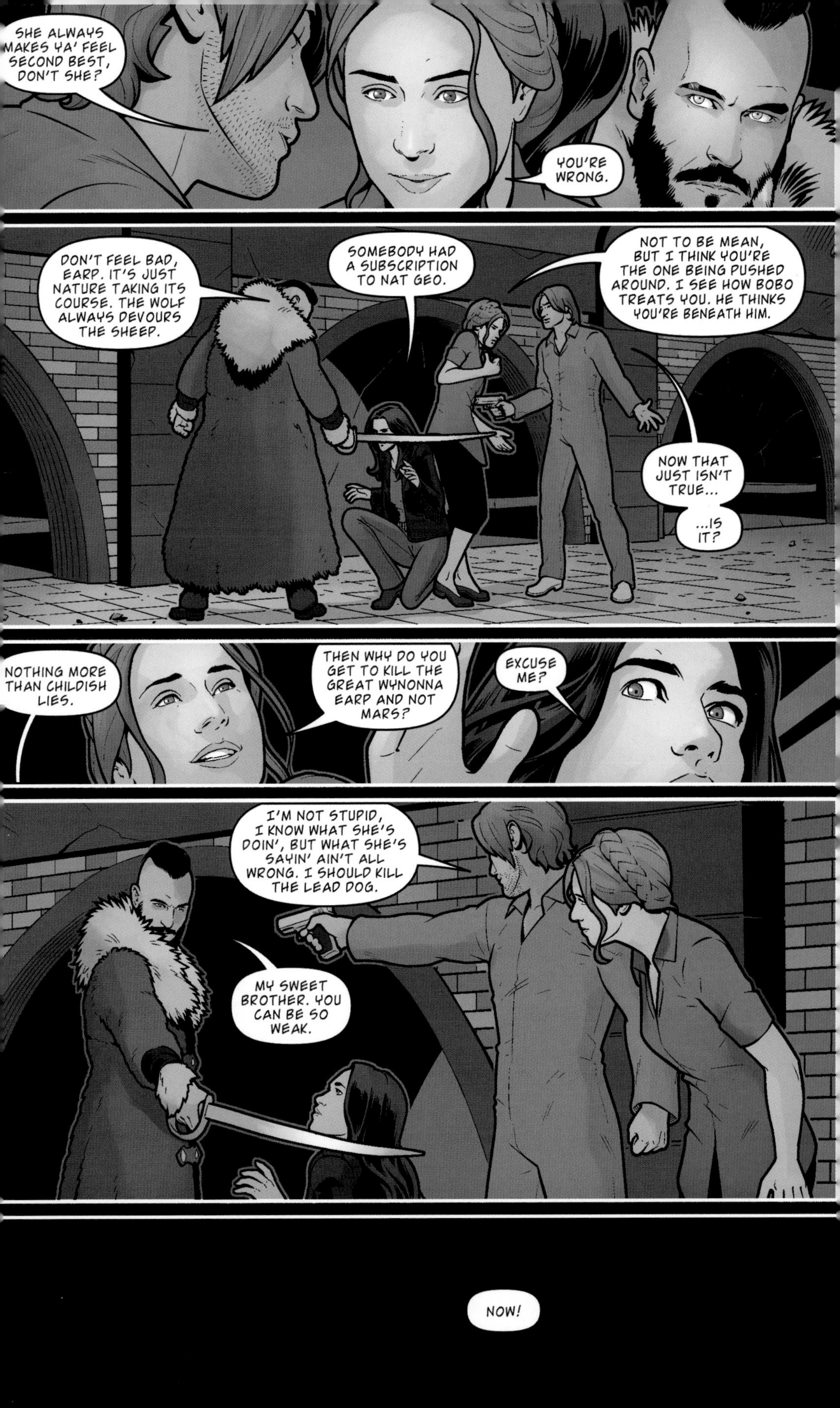

SHE ALWAYS MAKES YA' FEEL SECOND BEST, DON'T SHE?
YOU'RE WRONG.
DON'T FEEL BAD, EARP. IT'S JUST NATURE TAKING ITS COURSE. THE WOLF ALWAYS DEVOURS THE SHEEP.
SOMEBODY HAD A SUBSCRIPTION TO NAT GEO.
NOT TO BE MEAN, BUT I THINK YOU'RE THE ONE BEING PUSHED AROUND. I SEE HOW BOBO TREATS YOU. HE THINKS YOU'RE BENEATH HIM.
NOW THAT JUST ISN'T TRUE...
...IS IT?
NOTHING MORE THAN CHILDISH LIES.
THEN WHY DO YOU GET TO KILL THE GREAT WYNONNA EARP AND NOT MARS?
EXCUSE ME?
I'M NOT STUPID, I KNOW WHAT SHE'S DOIN', BUT WHAT SHE'S SAYIN' AIN'T ALL WRONG. I SHOULD KILL THE LEAD DOG.
MY SWEET BROTHER. YOU CAN BE SO WEAK.
NOW!

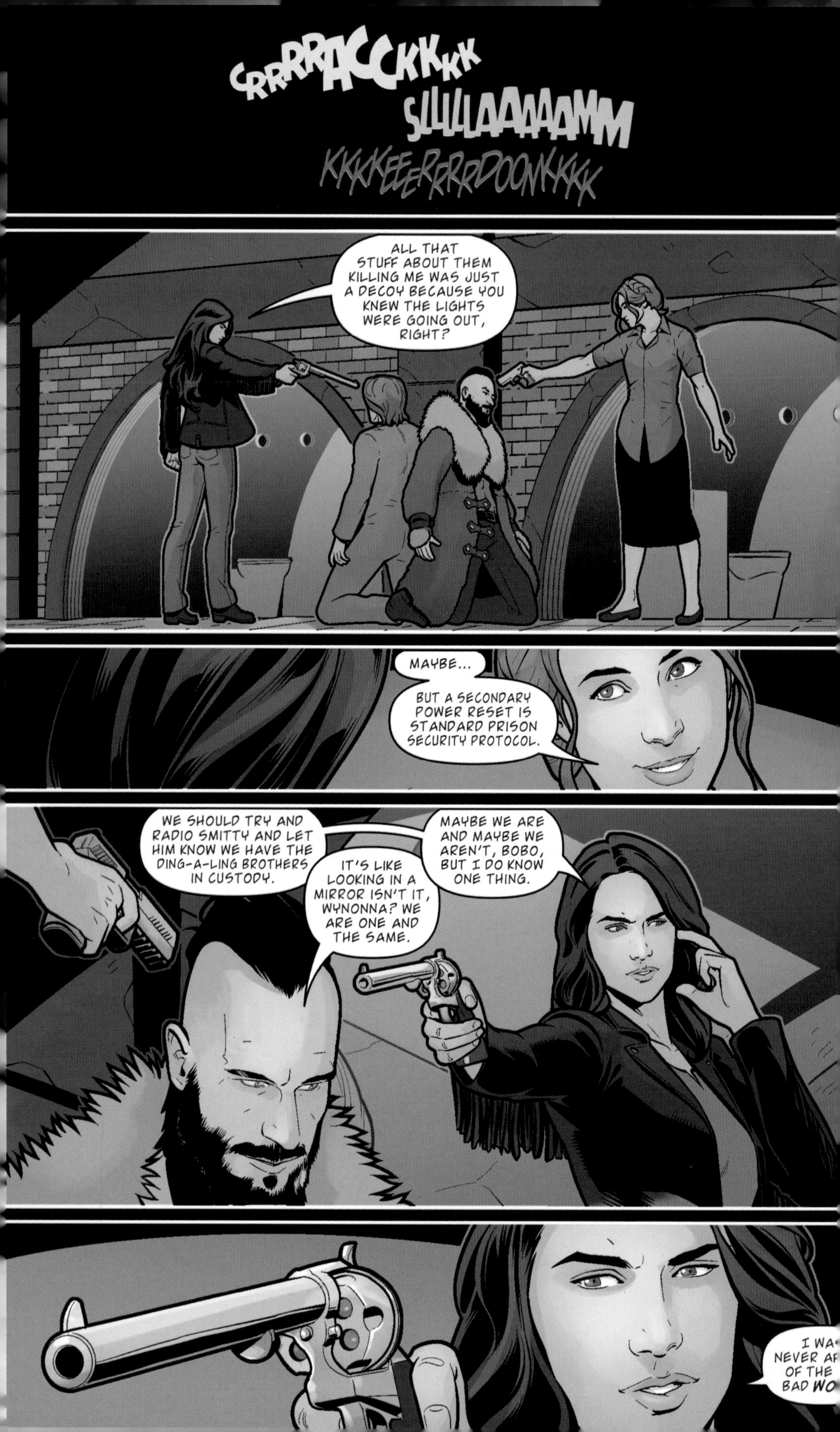
CRRRRACCKKKK
SLLLLAAAAAMM
KKKKEEERRRRDOONKKKK
ALL THAT STUFF ABOUT THEM KILLING ME WAS JUST A DECOY BECAUSE YOU KNEW THE LIGHTS WERE GOING OUT, RIGHT?
MAYBE...
BUT A SECONDARY POWER RESET IS STANDARD PRISON SECURITY PROTOCOL.
WE SHOULD TRY AND RADIO SMITTY AND LET HIM KNOW WE HAVE THE DING-A-LING BROTHERS IN CUSTODY.
IT'S LIKE LOOKING IN A MIRROR ISN'T IT, WYNONNA? WE ARE ONE AND THE SAME.
MAYBE WE ARE AND MAYBE WE AREN'T, BOBO, BUT I DO KNOW ONE THING.
I WA
NEVER A
OF THE
BAD WO

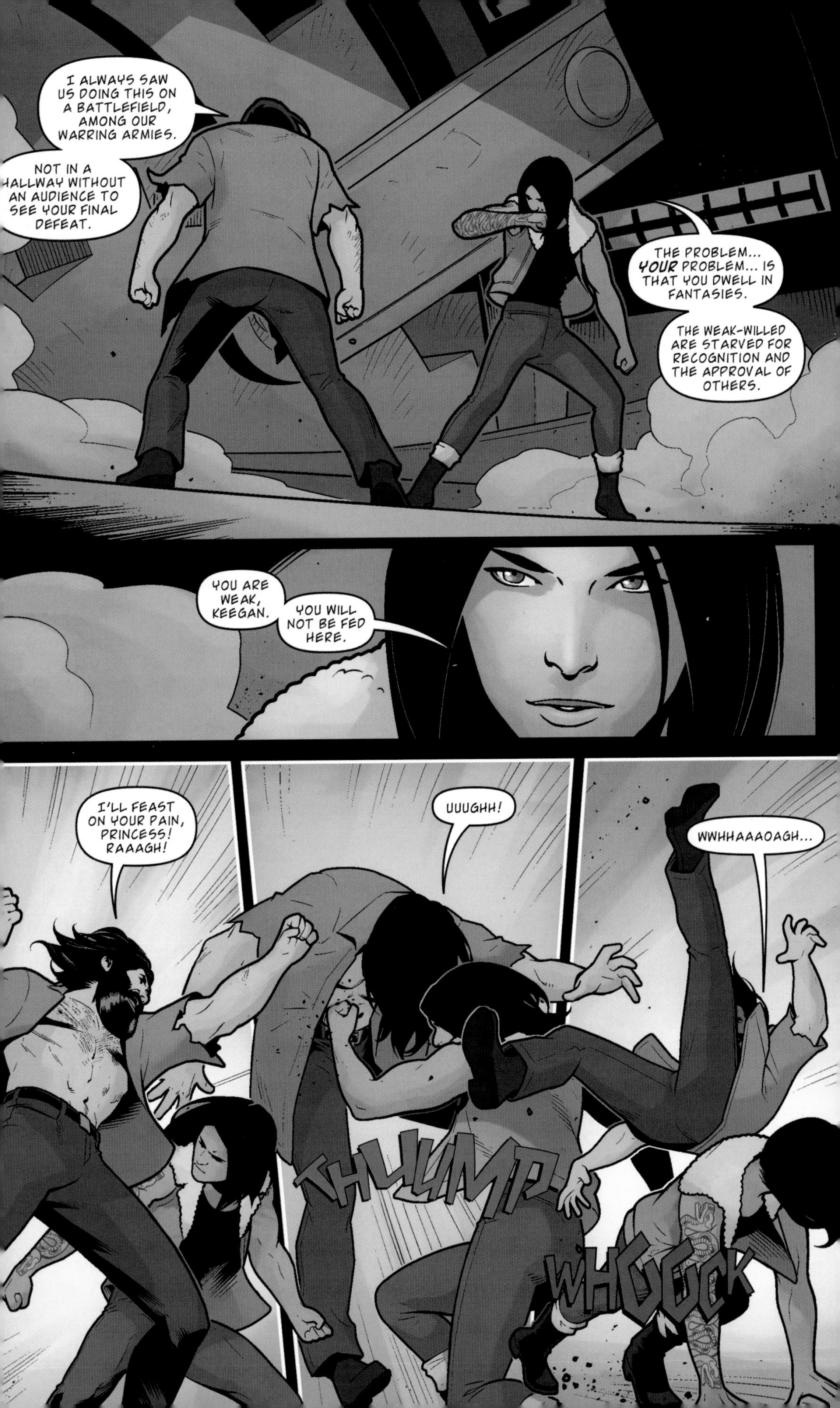
I ALWAYS SAW US DOING THIS ON A BATTLEFIELD, AMONG OUR WARRING ARMIES.
NOT IN A HALLWAY WITHOUT AN AUDIENCE TO SEE YOUR FINAL DEFEAT.
THE PROBLEM... YOUR PROBLEM... IS THAT YOU DWELL IN FANTASIES.
THE WEAK-WILLED ARE STARVED FOR RECOGNITION AND THE APPROVAL OF OTHERS.
YOU ARE WEAK, KEEGAN.
YOU WILL NOT BE FED HERE.
I'LL FEAST ON YOUR PAIN, PRINCESS! RAAAGH!
UUUGHH!
THUUMP
WWHHAAAOAGH...
WHOOCK

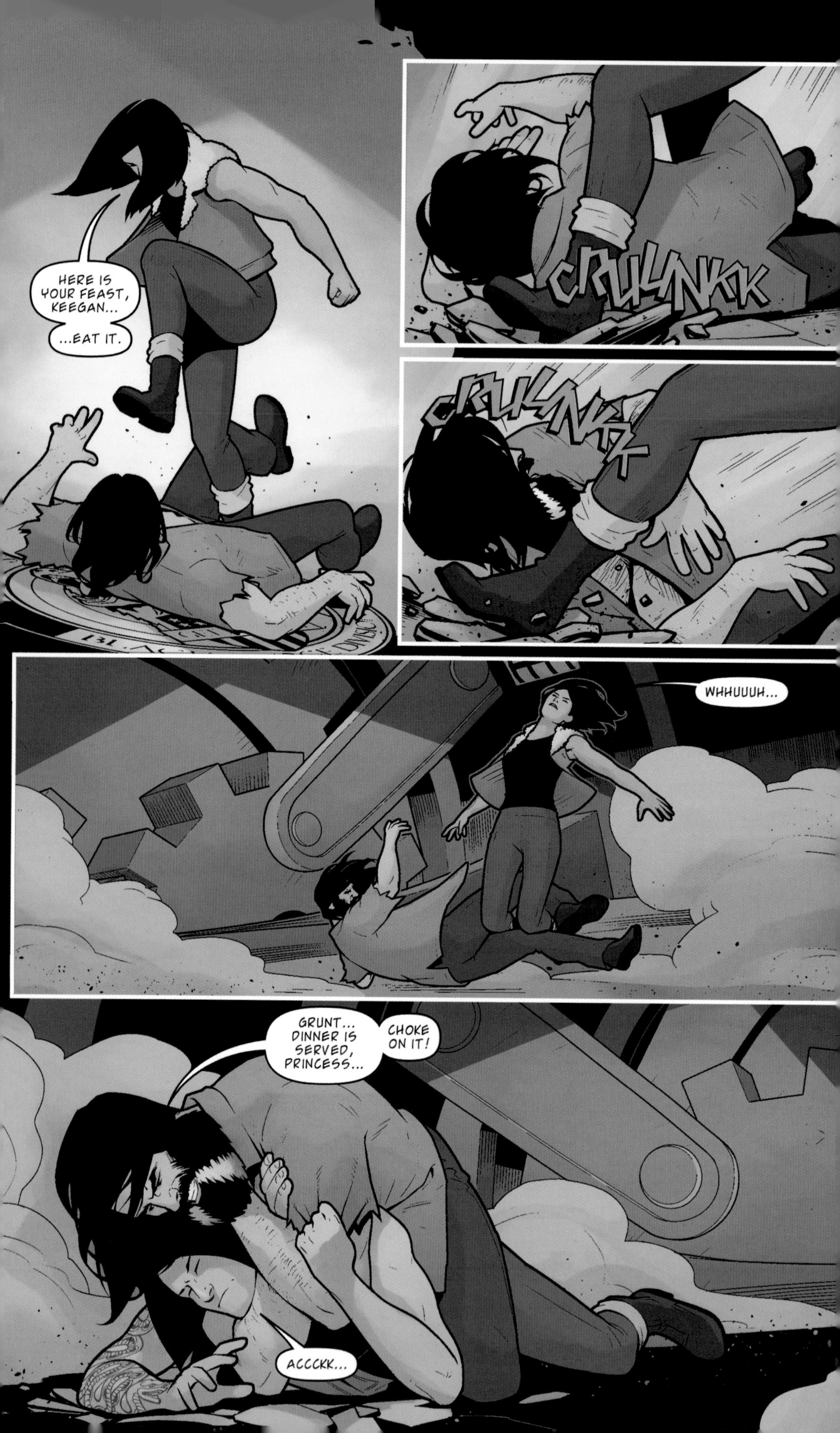
HERE IS YOUR FEAST, KEEGAN...
...EAT IT.
CRUNKK
CRUNKK
WHHUUUH...
GRUNT... DINNER IS SERVED, PRINCESS...
CHOKE ON IT!
ACCCKK...

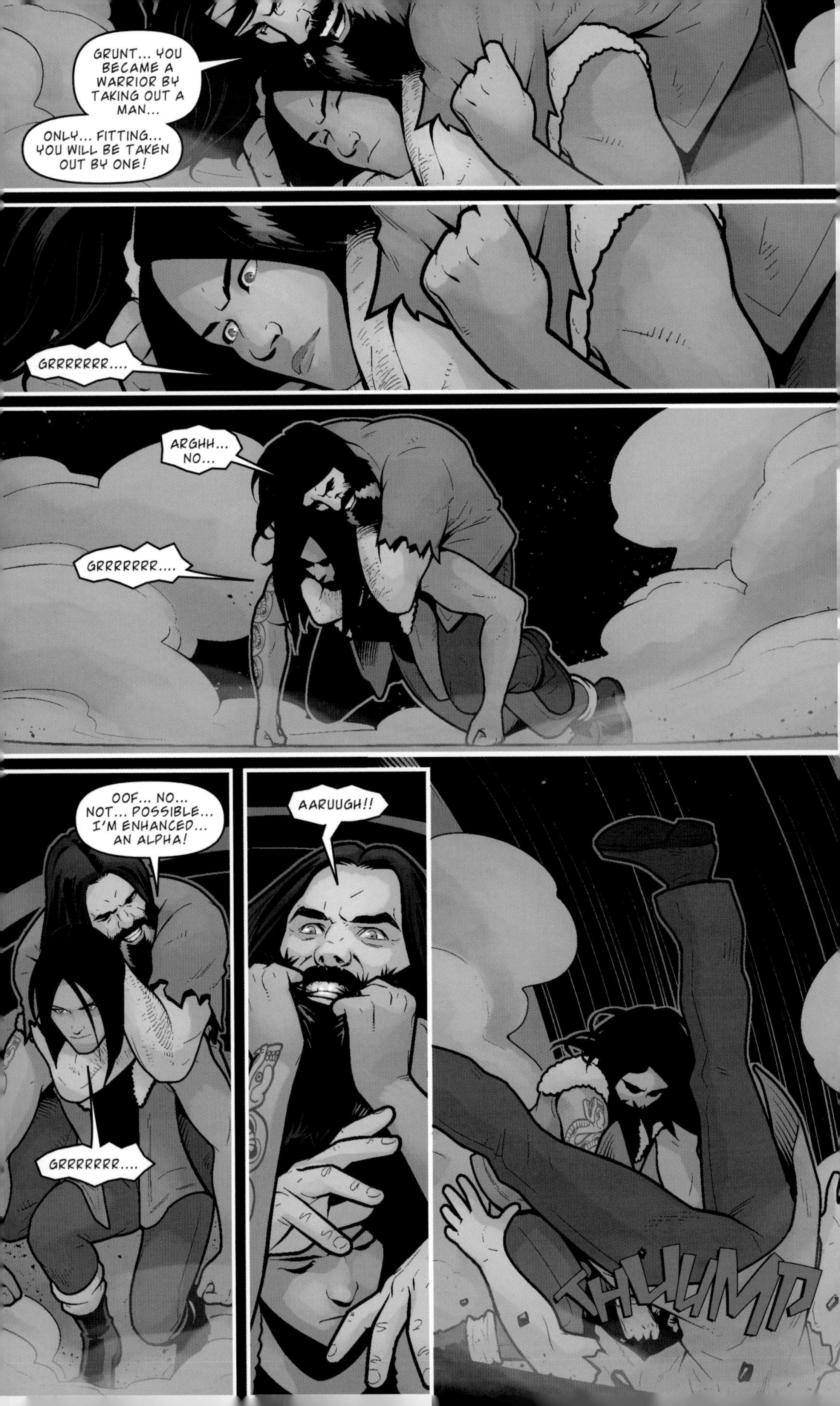
GRUNT... YOU BECAME A WARRIOR BY TAKING OUT A MAN...
ONLY... FITTING... YOU WILL BE TAKEN OUT BY ONE!
GRRRRRRR....
ARGHH... NO...
GRRRRRRR....
OOF... NO... NOT... POSSIBLE... I'M ENHANCED... AN ALPHA!
GRRRRRRR....
AARUUGH!!
THUUMP!

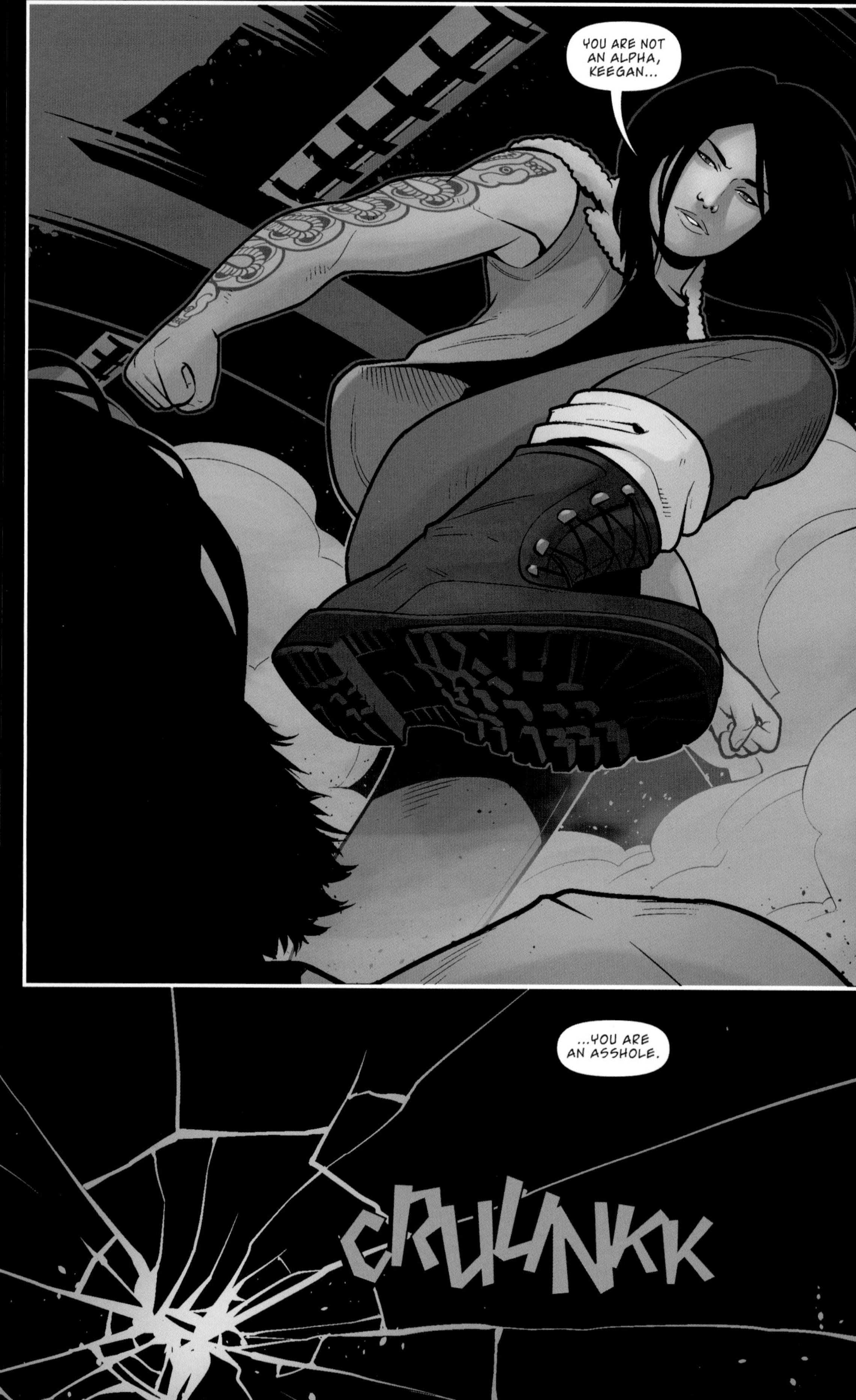
YOU ARE NOT AN ALPHA, KEEGAN...
...YOU ARE AN ASSHOLE.
CRUNKK

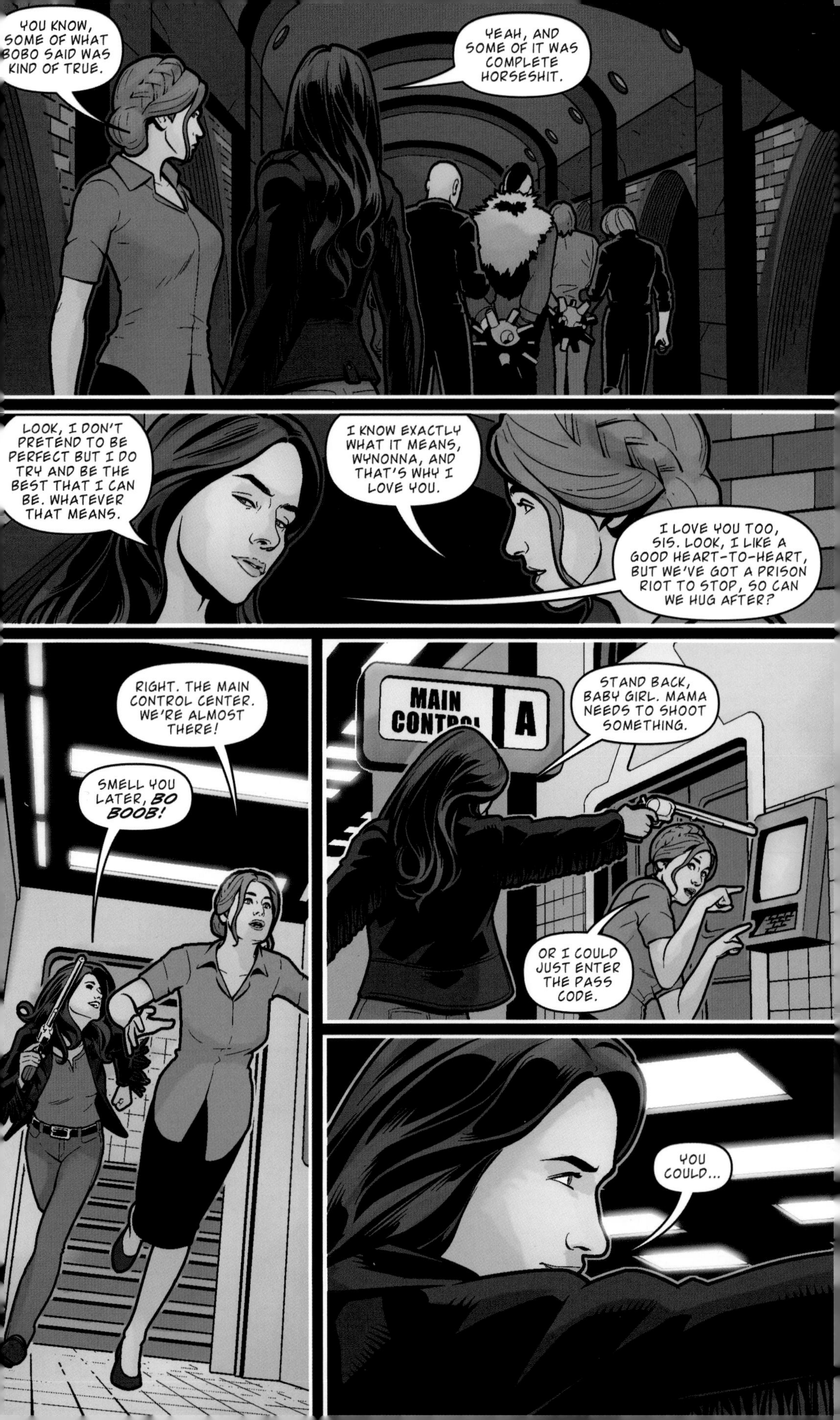
YOU KNOW, SOME OF WHAT BOBO SAID WAS KIND OF TRUE.
YEAH, AND SOME OF IT WAS COMPLETE HORSESHIT.
LOOK, I DON'T PRETEND TO BE PERFECT BUT I DO TRY AND BE THE BEST THAT I CAN BE. WHATEVER THAT MEANS.
I KNOW EXACTLY WHAT IT MEANS, WYNONNA, AND THAT'S WHY I LOVE YOU.
I LOVE YOU TOO, SIS. LOOK, I LIKE A GOOD HEART-TO-HEART, BUT WE'VE GOT A PRISON RIOT TO STOP, SO CAN WE HUG AFTER?
RIGHT. THE MAIN CONTROL CENTER. WE'RE ALMOST THERE!
SMELL YOU LATER, ***BO BOOB!***
A
STAND BACK, BABY GIRL. MAMA NEEDS TO SHOOT SOMETHING.
OR I COULD JUST ENTER THE PASS CODE.
YOU COULD...

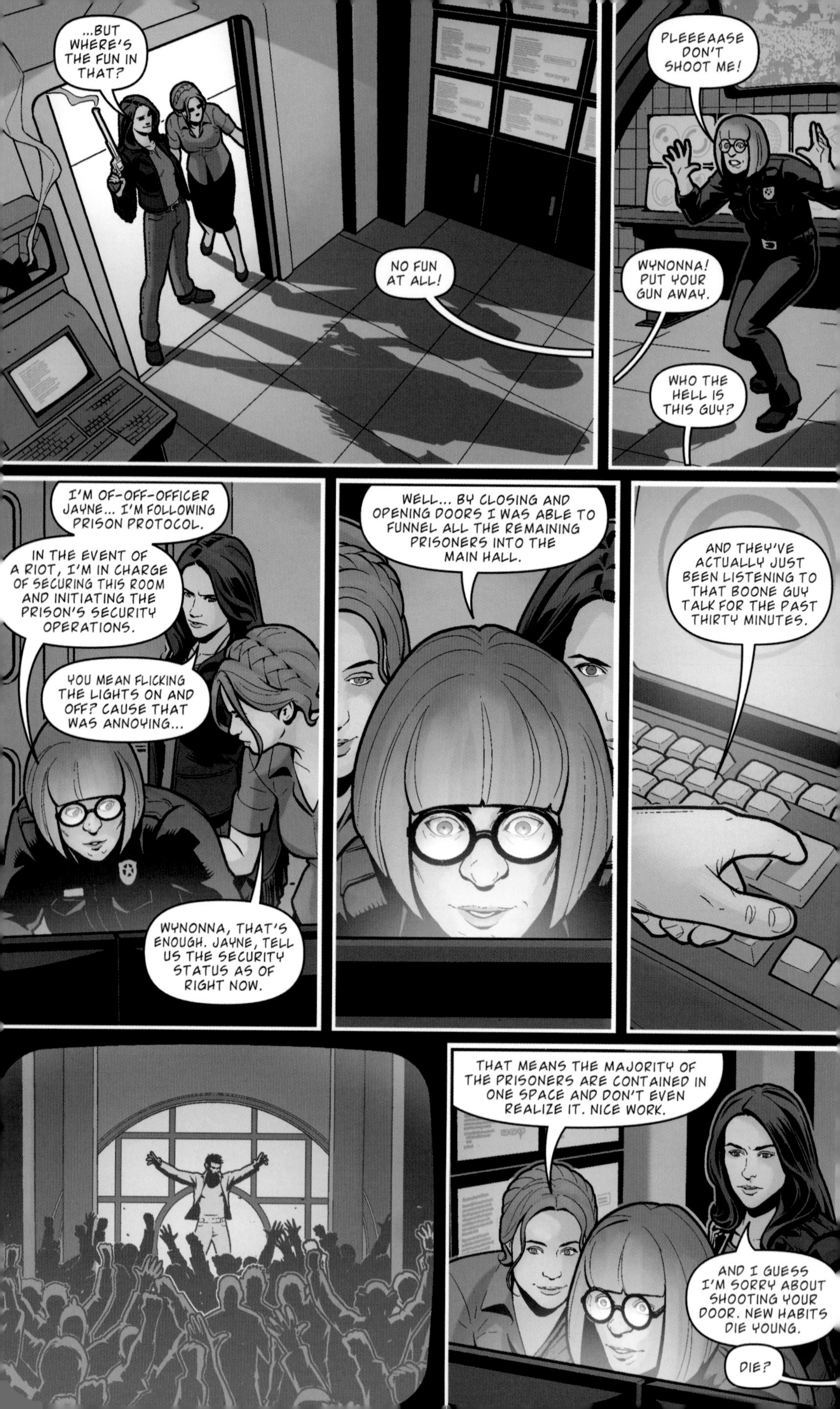
...BUT WHERE'S THE FUN IN THAT?
NO FUN AT ALL!
PLEEEAASE DON'T SHOOT ME!
WYNONNA! PUT YOUR GUN AWAY.
WHO THE HELL IS THIS GUY?
I'M OF-OFF-OFFICER JAYNE... I'M FOLLOWING PRISON PROTOCOL.
IN THE EVENT OF A RIOT, I'M IN CHARGE OF SECURING THIS ROOM AND INITIATING THE PRISON'S SECURITY OPERATIONS.
YOU MEAN FLICKING THE LIGHTS ON AND OFF? CAUSE THAT WAS ANNOYING...
WYNONNA, THAT'S ENOUGH. JAYNE, TELL US THE SECURITY STATUS AS OF RIGHT NOW.
WELL... BY CLOSING AND OPENING DOORS I WAS ABLE TO FUNNEL ALL THE REMAINING PRISONERS INTO THE MAIN HALL.
AND THEY'VE ACTUALLY JUST BEEN LISTENING TO THAT BOONE GUY TALK FOR THE PAST THIRTY MINUTES.
THAT MEANS THE MAJORITY OF THE PRISONERS ARE CONTAINED IN ONE SPACE AND DON'T EVEN REALIZE IT. NICE WORK.
AND I GUESS I'M SORRY ABOUT SHOOTING YOUR DOOR. NEW HABITS DIE YOUNG.
DIE?

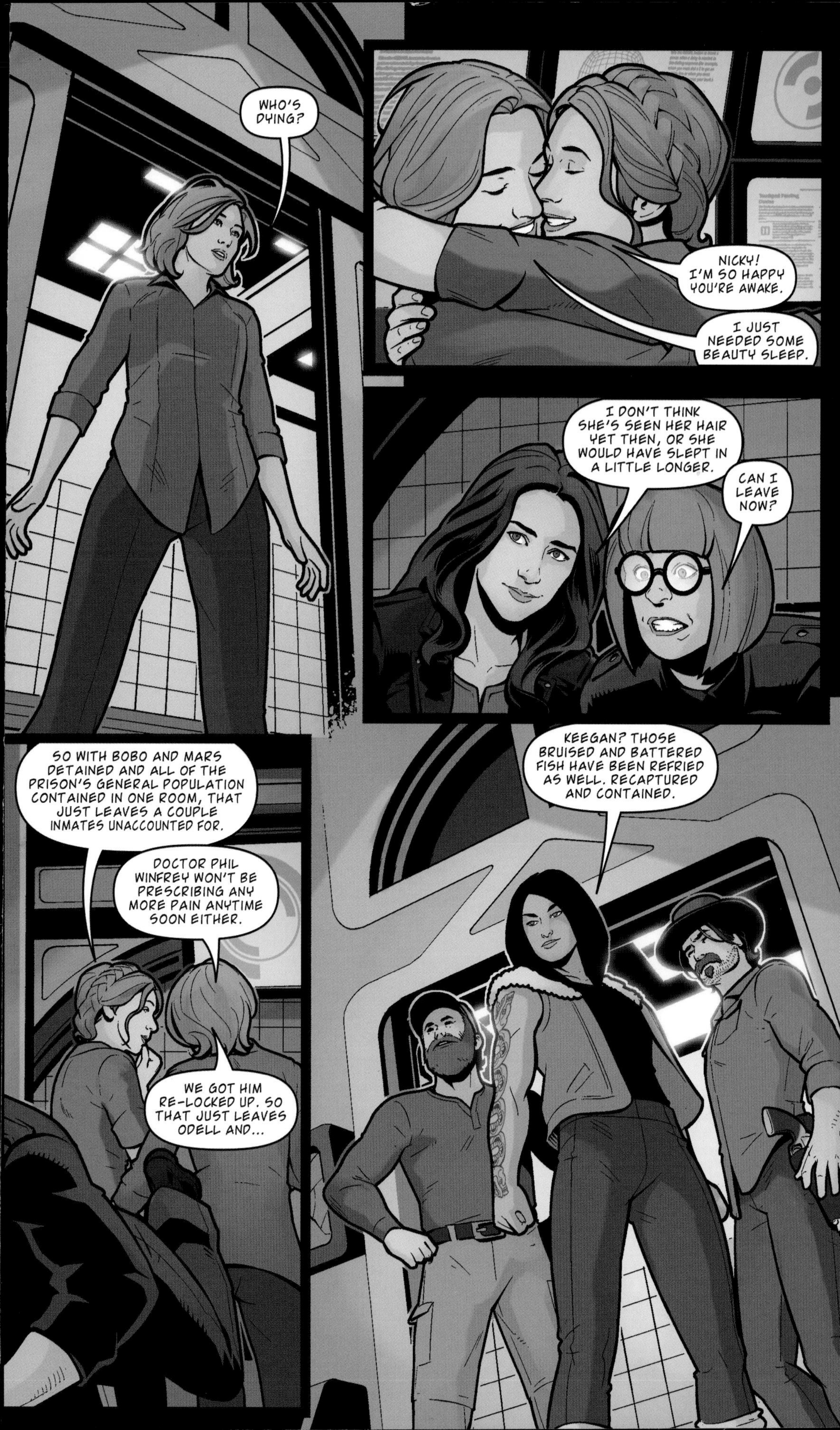
WHO'S DYING?
NICKY! I'M SO HAPPY YOU'RE AWAKE.
I JUST NEEDED SOME BEAUTY SLEEP.
I DON'T THINK SHE'S SEEN HER HAIR YET THEN, OR SHE WOULD HAVE SLEPT IN A LITTLE LONGER.
CAN I LEAVE NOW?
SO WITH BOBO AND MARS DETAINED AND ALL OF THE PRISON'S GENERAL POPULATION CONTAINED IN ONE ROOM, THAT JUST LEAVES A COUPLE INMATES UNACCOUNTED FOR.
DOCTOR PHIL WINFREY WON'T BE PRESCRIBING ANY MORE PAIN ANYTIME SOON EITHER.
WE GOT HIM RE-LOCKED UP. SO THAT JUST LEAVES ODELL AND...
KEEGAN? THOSE BRUISED AND BATTERED FISH HAVE BEEN REFRIED AS WELL. RECAPTURED AND CONTAINED.

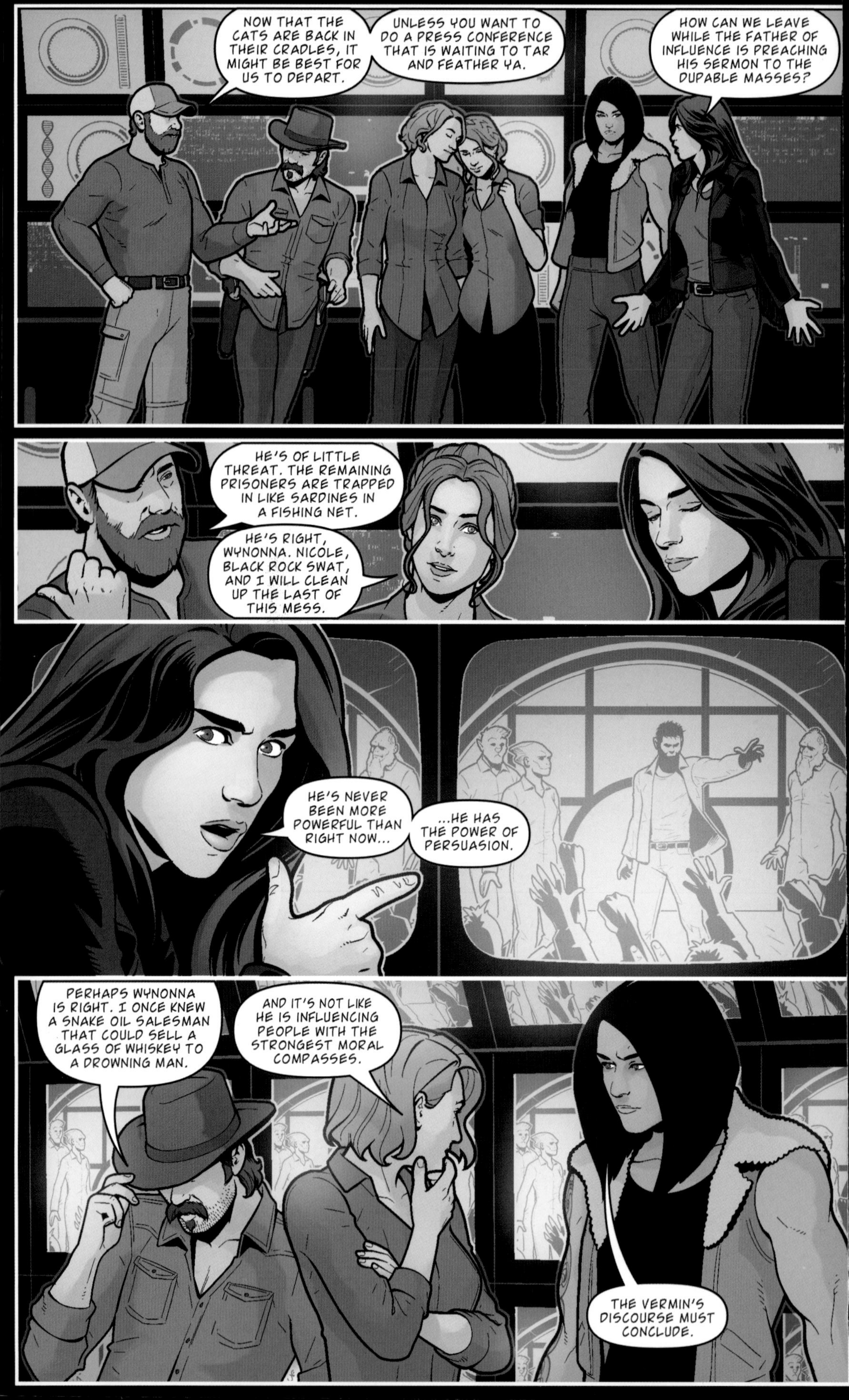
NOW THAT THE CATS ARE BACK IN THEIR CRADLES, IT MIGHT BE BEST FOR US TO DEPART.
UNLESS YOU WANT TO DO A PRESS CONFERENCE THAT IS WAITING TO TAR AND FEATHER YA.
HOW CAN WE LEAVE WHILE THE FATHER OF INFLUENCE IS PREACHING HIS SERMON TO THE DUPABLE MASSES?
HE'S OF LITTLE THREAT. THE REMAINING PRISONERS ARE TRAPPED IN LIKE SARDINES IN A FISHING NET.
HE'S RIGHT, WYNONNA. NICOLE, BLACK ROCK SWAT, AND I WILL CLEAN UP THE LAST OF THIS MESS.
HE'S NEVER BEEN MORE POWERFUL THAN RIGHT NOW...
...HE HAS THE POWER OF PERSUASION.
PERHAPS WYNONNA IS RIGHT. I ONCE KNEW A SNAKE OIL SALESMAN THAT COULD SELL A GLASS OF WHISKEY TO A DROWNING MAN.
AND IT'S NOT LIKE HE IS INFLUENCING PEOPLE WITH THE STRONGEST MORAL COMPASSES.
THE VERMIN'S DISCOURSE MUST CONCLUDE.

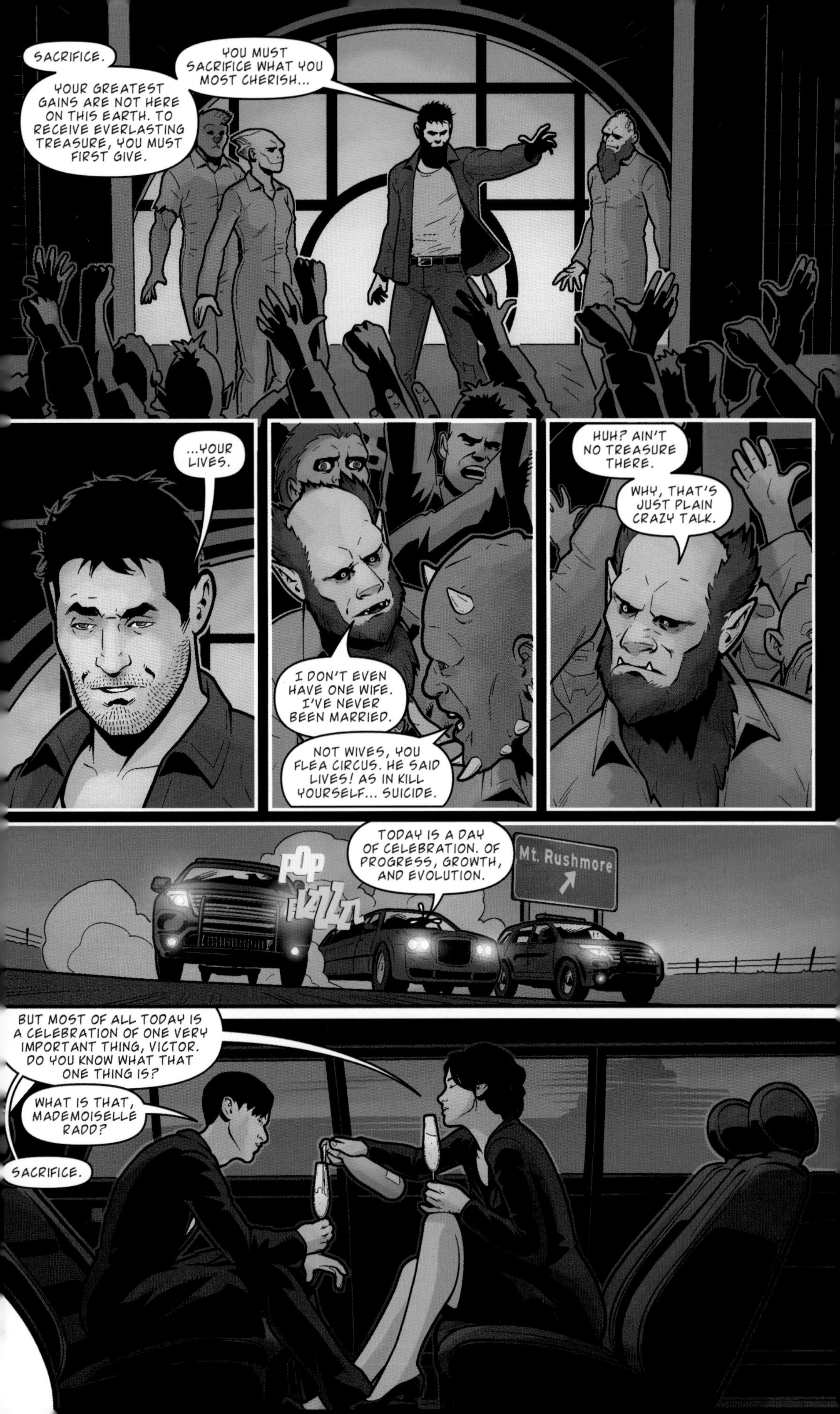
SACRIFICE.
YOUR GREATEST GAINS ARE NOT HERE ON THIS EARTH. TO RECEIVE EVERLASTING TREASURE, YOU MUST FIRST GIVE.
YOU MUST SACRIFICE WHAT YOU MOST CHERISH...
...YOUR LIVES.
I DON'T EVEN HAVE ONE WIFE. I'VE NEVER BEEN MARRIED.
NOT WIVES, YOU FLEA CIRCUS. HE SAID LIVES! AS IN KILL YOURSELF... SUICIDE.
HUH? AIN'T NO TREASURE THERE.
WHY, THAT'S JUST PLAIN CRAZY TALK.
POP
FZZZZT
TODAY IS A DAY OF CELEBRATION. OF PROGRESS, GROWTH, AND EVOLUTION.
Mt. Rushmore
BUT MOST OF ALL TODAY IS A CELEBRATION OF ONE VERY IMPORTANT THING, VICTOR. DO YOU KNOW WHAT THAT ONE THING IS?
WHAT IS THAT, MADEMOISELLE RADD?
SACRIFICE.

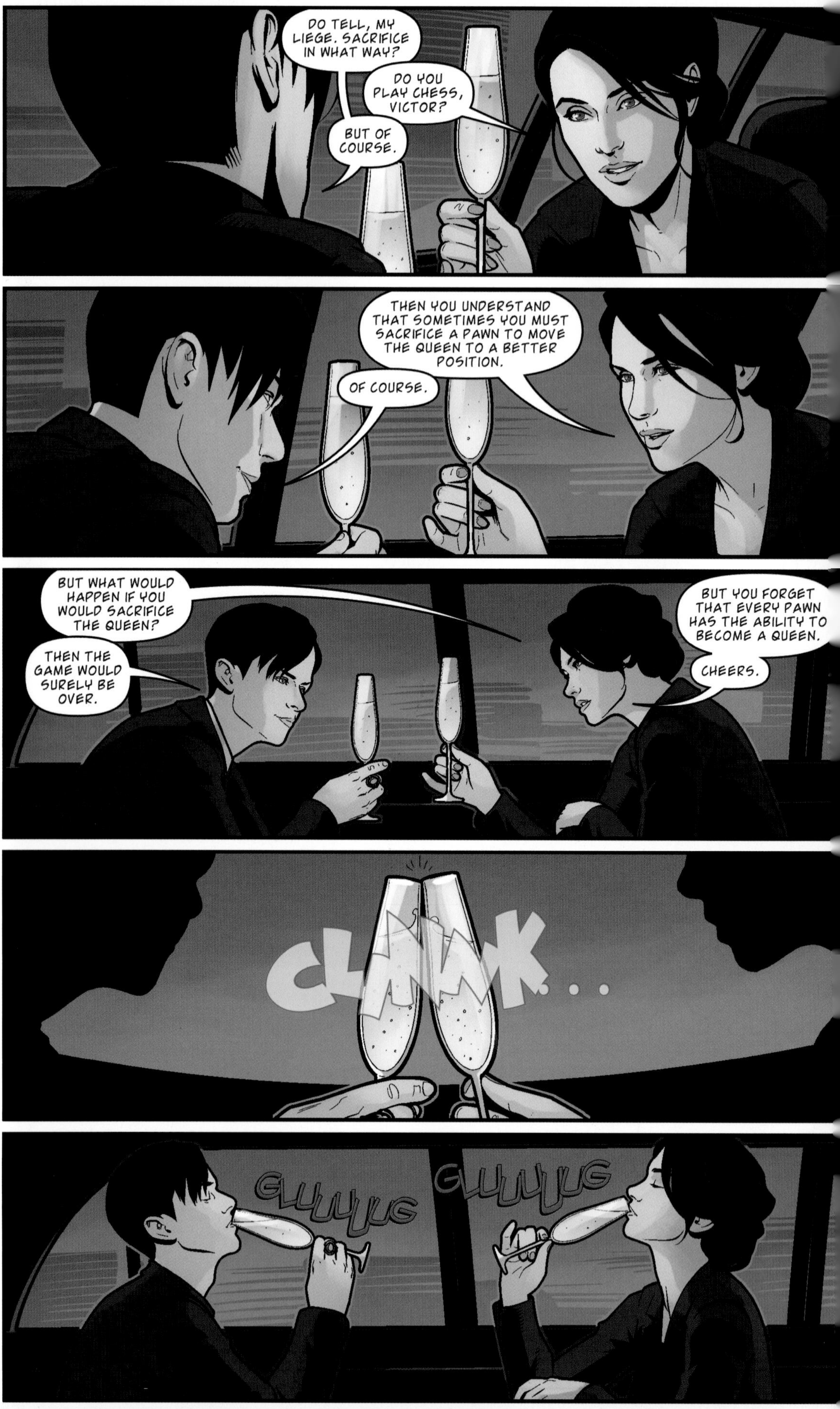
DO TELL, MY LIEGE. SACRIFICE IN WHAT WAY?
DO YOU PLAY CHESS, VICTOR?
BUT OF COURSE.
THEN YOU UNDERSTAND THAT SOMETIMES YOU MUST SACRIFICE A PAWN TO MOVE THE QUEEN TO A BETTER POSITION.
OF COURSE.
BUT WHAT WOULD HAPPEN IF YOU WOULD SACRIFICE THE QUEEN?
THEN THE GAME WOULD SURELY BE OVER.
BUT YOU FORGET THAT EVERY PAWN HAS THE ABILITY TO BECOME A QUEEN.
CHEERS.
CLINK...
GLUUUUUG
GLUUUUUG

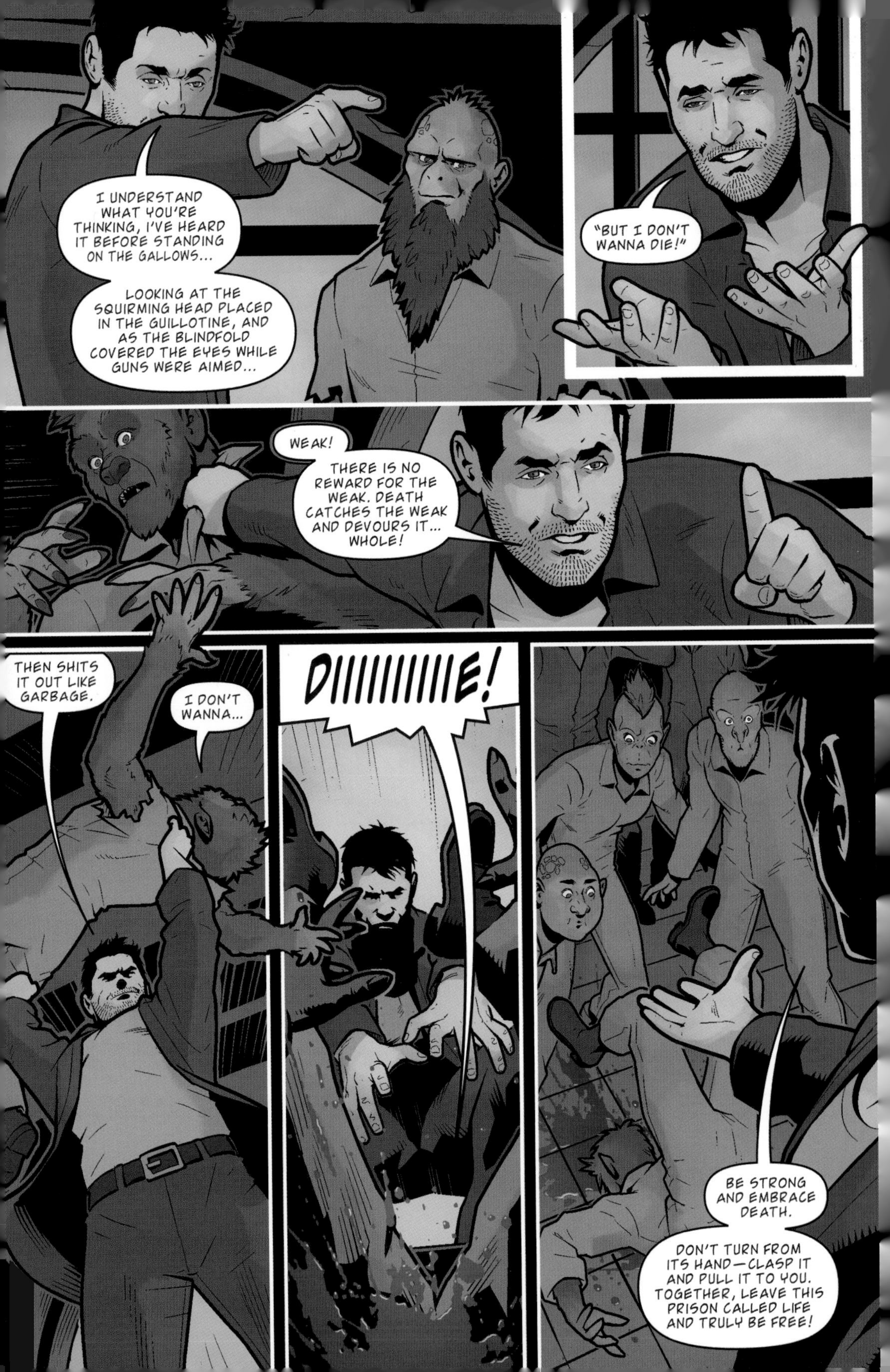
I UNDERSTAND WHAT YOU'RE THINKING, I'VE HEARD IT BEFORE STANDING ON THE GALLOWS...
LOOKING AT THE SQUIRMING HEAD PLACED IN THE GUILLOTINE, AND AS THE BLINDFOLD COVERED THE EYES WHILE GUNS WERE AIMED...
"BUT I DON'T WANNA DIE!"
WEAK!
THERE IS NO REWARD FOR THE WEAK. DEATH CATCHES THE WEAK AND DEVOURS IT... WHOLE!
THEN SHITS IT OUT LIKE GARBAGE.
I DON'T WANNA...
DIIIIIIIIIIE!
BE STRONG AND EMBRACE DEATH.
DON'T TURN FROM ITS HAND—CLASP IT AND PULL IT TO YOU. TOGETHER, LEAVE THIS PRISON CALLED LIFE AND TRULY BE FREE!

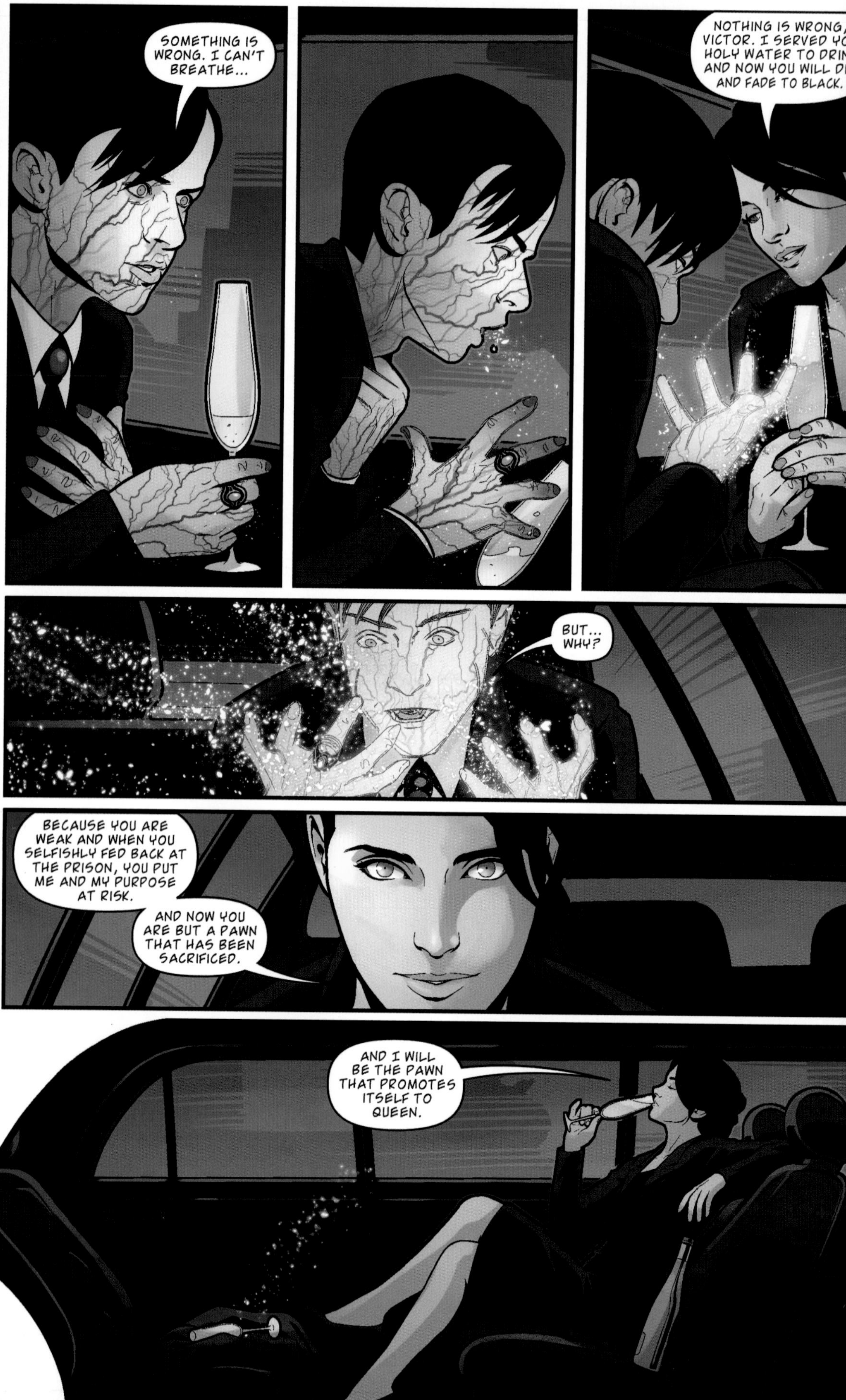
SOMETHING IS WRONG. I CAN'T BREATHE...
NOTHING IS WRONG, VICTOR. I SERVED YO HOLY WATER TO DRIN AND NOW YOU WILL D AND FADE TO BLACK.
BUT... WHY?
BECAUSE YOU ARE WEAK AND WHEN YOU SELFISHLY FED BACK AT THE PRISON, YOU PUT ME AND MY PURPOSE AT RISK.
AND NOW YOU ARE BUT A PAWN THAT HAS BEEN SACRIFICED.
AND I WILL BE THE PAWN THAT PROMOTES ITSELF TO QUEEN.

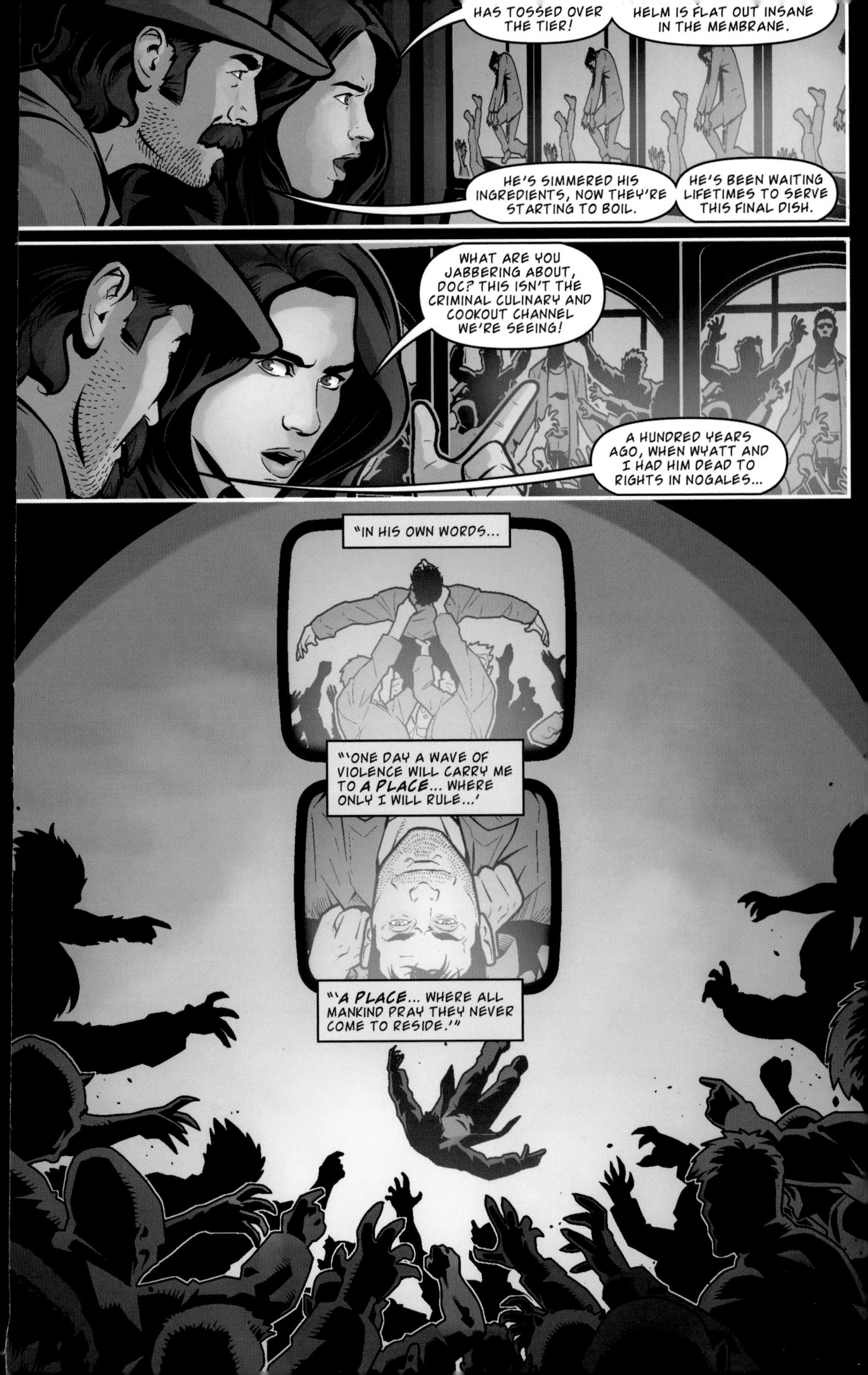
HAS TOSSED OVER THE TIER!
HELM IS FLAT OUT INSANE IN THE MEMBRANE.
HE'S SIMMERED HIS INGREDIENTS, NOW THEY'RE STARTING TO BOIL.
HE'S BEEN WAITING LIFETIMES TO SERVE THIS FINAL DISH.
WHAT ARE YOU JABBERING ABOUT, DOC? THIS ISN'T THE CRIMINAL CULINARY AND COOKOUT CHANNEL WE'RE SEEING!
A HUNDRED YEARS AGO, WHEN WYATT AND I HAD HIM DEAD TO RIGHTS IN NOGALES...
"IN HIS OWN WORDS...
"'ONE DAY A WAVE OF VIOLENCE WILL CARRY ME TO *A PLACE*... WHERE ONLY I WILL RULE...'
"'*A PLACE*... WHERE ALL MANKIND PRAY THEY NEVER COME TO RESIDE.'"

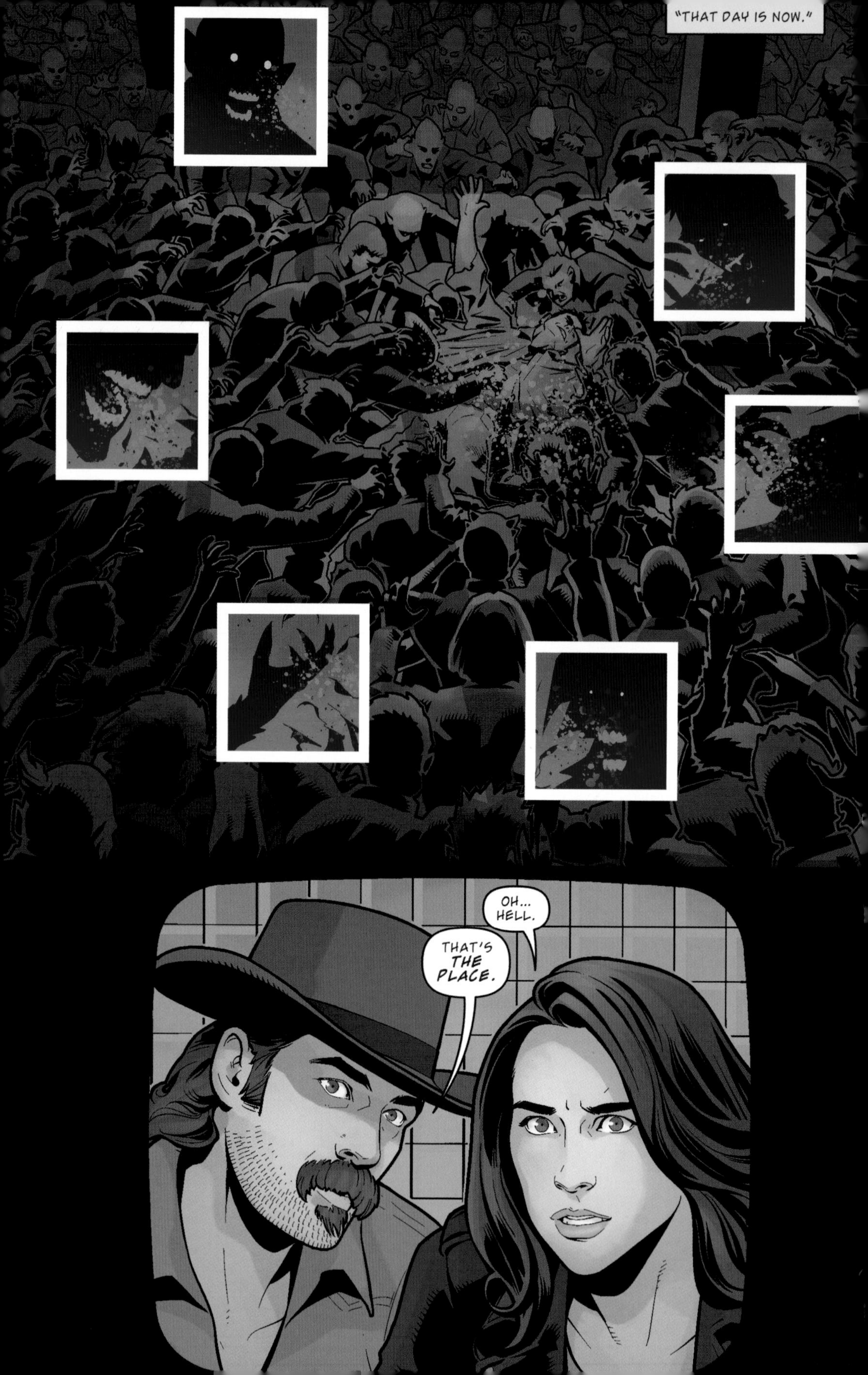
"THAT DAY IS NOW."
OH... HELL.
THAT'S THE PLACE.

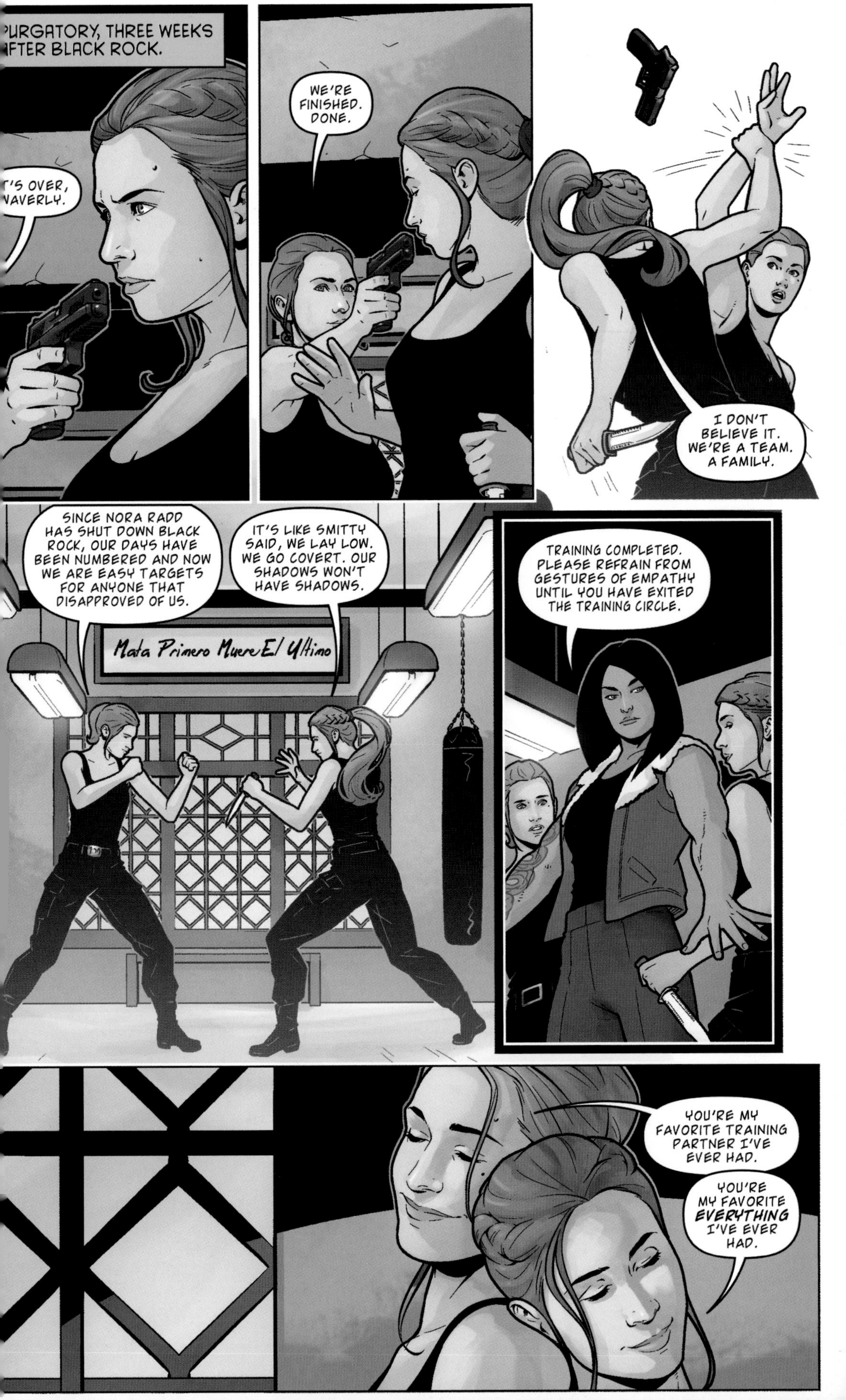
PURGATORY, THREE WEEKS AFTER BLACK ROCK.
IT'S OVER, WAVERLY.
WE'RE FINISHED. DONE.
I DON'T BELIEVE IT. WE'RE A TEAM. A FAMILY.
SINCE NORA RADD HAS SHUT DOWN BLACK ROCK, OUR DAYS HAVE BEEN NUMBERED AND NOW WE ARE EASY TARGETS FOR ANYONE THAT DISAPPROVED OF US.
IT'S LIKE SMITTY SAID, WE LAY LOW. WE GO COVERT. OUR SHADOWS WON'T HAVE SHADOWS.
Mata Primero Muere El Ultimo
TRAINING COMPLETED. PLEASE REFRAIN FROM GESTURES OF EMPATHY UNTIL YOU HAVE EXITED THE TRAINING CIRCLE.
YOU'RE MY FAVORITE TRAINING PARTNER I'VE EVER HAD.
YOU'RE MY FAVORITE *EVERYTHING* I'VE EVER HAD.

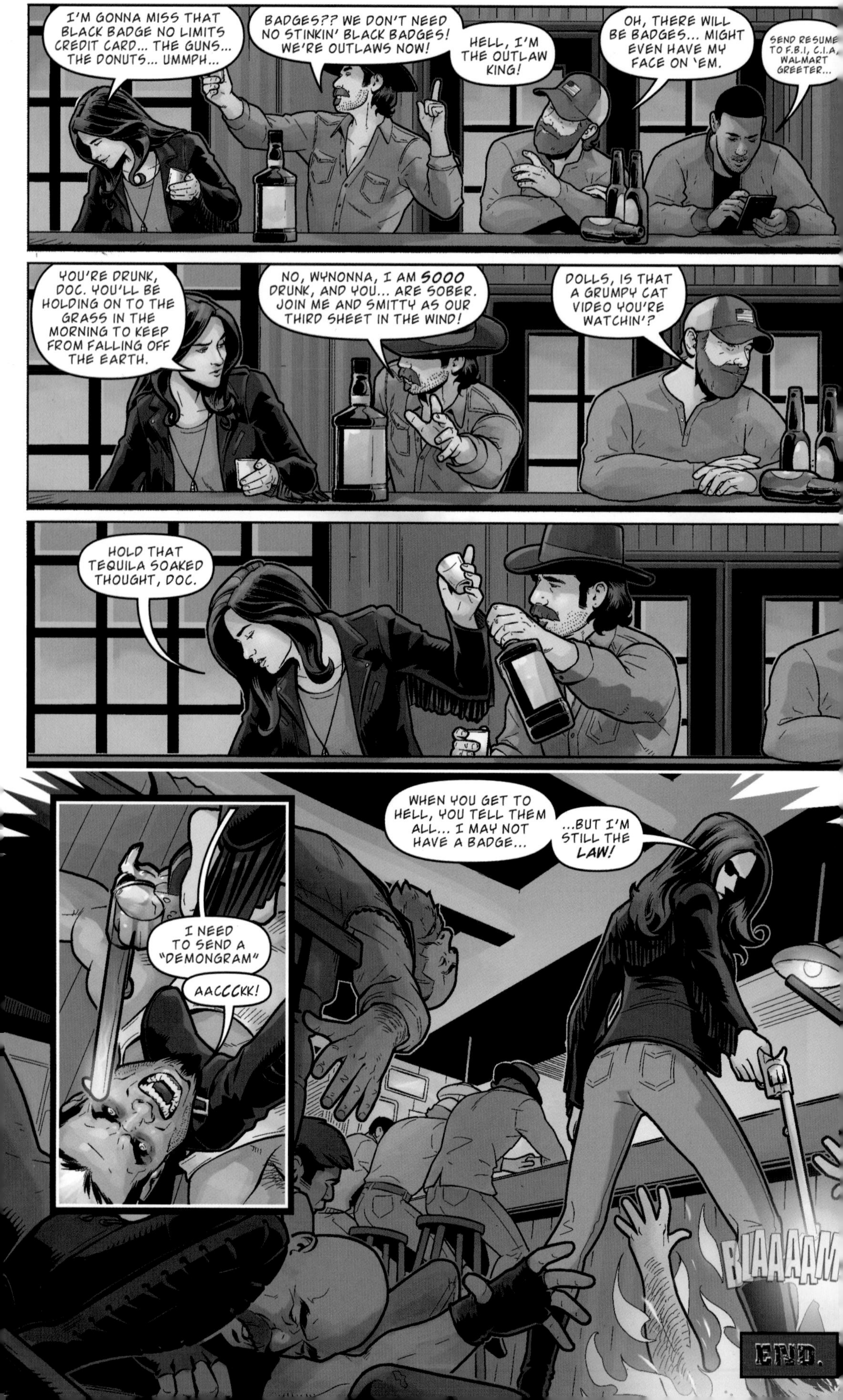
I'M GONNA MISS THAT BLACK BADGE NO LIMITS CREDIT CARD... THE GUNS... THE DONUTS... UMMPH...
BADGES?? WE DON'T NEED NO STINKIN' BLACK BADGES! WE'RE OUTLAWS NOW!
HELL, I'M THE OUTLAW KING!
OH, THERE WILL BE BADGES... MIGHT EVEN HAVE MY FACE ON 'EM.
SEND RESUME TO F.B.I, C.I.A, WALMART GREETER...
YOU'RE DRUNK, DOC. YOU'LL BE HOLDING ON TO THE GRASS IN THE MORNING TO KEEP FROM FALLING OFF THE EARTH.
NO, WYNONNA, I AM SOOO DRUNK, AND YOU... ARE SOBER. JOIN ME AND SMITTY AS OUR THIRD SHEET IN THE WIND!
DOLLS, IS THAT A GRUMPY CAT VIDEO YOU'RE WATCHIN'?
HOLD THAT TEQUILA SOAKED THOUGHT, DOC.
I NEED TO SEND A "DEMONGRAM"
AACCCKK!
WHEN YOU GET TO HELL, YOU TELL THEM ALL... I MAY NOT HAVE A BADGE...
...BUT I'M STILL THE LAW!
BLAAAAM
END.

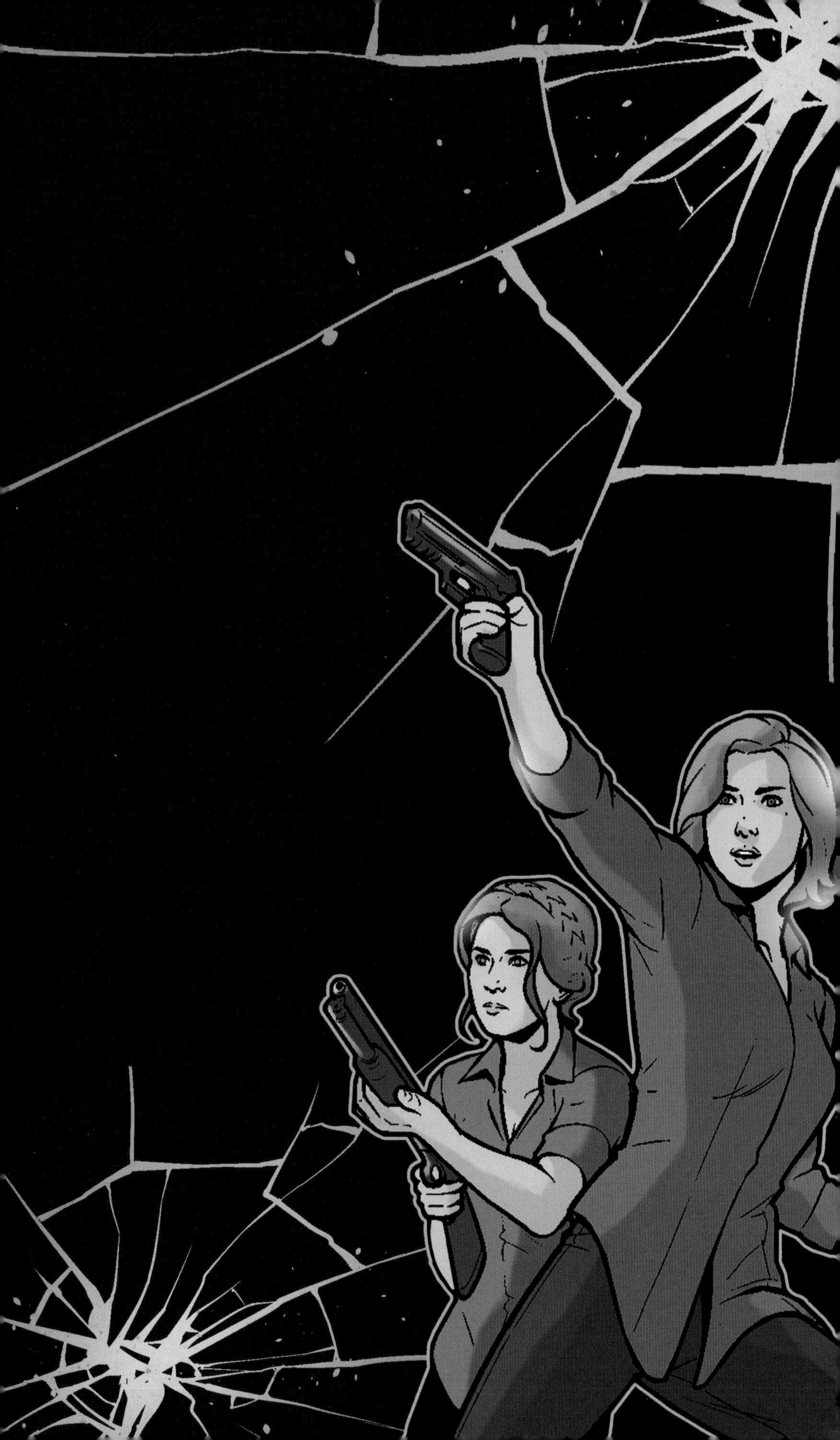

Doc Holliday: High Noon

By Tim Rozon

His eyes are permanently squinted from the sun and he strains them to see past the bottom of the pencil-curled brim of his old worn hat.

His throat is burned and heavy with smoke from the chewed cigarillo that dangles from the corner of his mouth, irritating the consumption that is killing him with his every breath.

He spits a mix of whiskey, grit, and chad, as he digs his dirty boot into the dirtier hard ground beneath his foot. It hurts his frail bones to push into the dirt, but he needs the footing to help him balance. He is ever slightly drunk and it is well before noon.

The palm of his shaky right hand gently hovers over the pearl handle of his .41 Long Colt Thunderer pistol. It's a feeling he is more than familiar with. Some would even say the only time he did feel at all is when he drew said pistol from his holster.

He will need to feel today.

He is a professional gambler by trade, poker his game, but he is known more now for the efficacy of his shot as the deadliest gunslinger that ever walked the earth. Oddly enough, he actually started out as a dentist. Hence he earned the nickname of "Doc," but most people either way knew him as Holliday.

Standing just fifty paces from him stands none other than the notorious Johnny Ringo of the outlaw Cochise County Cowboys. Johnny has one sole purpose today and that is to outdraw, out shoot, and outlive Mr. Holliday. Ringo is a hard man and hell bent on living or dying that way. Ringo and Holliday have a history and when it comes to hard men, having a history means something.

One of them will die today.

Johnny Ringo is in the prime of a young man's life. He is a fierce, bloodthirsty, and menacing loudmouth of a man. He is a perfect blend of viciousness and devilry. It is said he has killed seven men. He plans to kill one more today.

Doc is a dying man. His lungs failing him. His liver poisoning him. He is as tired as he is bitter and knows that no salvation awaits him.

This, however, doesn't mean Doc will go down easy and he has made no plans to meet his maker today

The two men lock eyes.

Neither willing to blink.

A thousand words said within the deadliness of the stare shared between them.

The smoke from Doc's cigarillo dances across his worn out eyes.

Johnny Ringo draws fast and hard...

Doc has drawn fast and true.

They both know.

Johnny Ringo falls first to his knees in disbelief, that an old dying man has out drawn him. Then he topples over to the hard ground, where he knows he will take his last breath. His only comfort is the warm blood oozing from his belly. Ringo forces a glance up to Doc.

Doc is unfazed, uncaring, and unmoved. Doc Holliday is a stone cold killer and he has been here before many times.

"How is it that through your bleedin' lungs... you out drew me?" gasped Ringo.

Doc Holliday looked down at the dying Ringo and replied, "Because you care too much about livin', son."

Doc took one last drag of his cigarillo and as he exhaled he muttered to himself, "I don't."

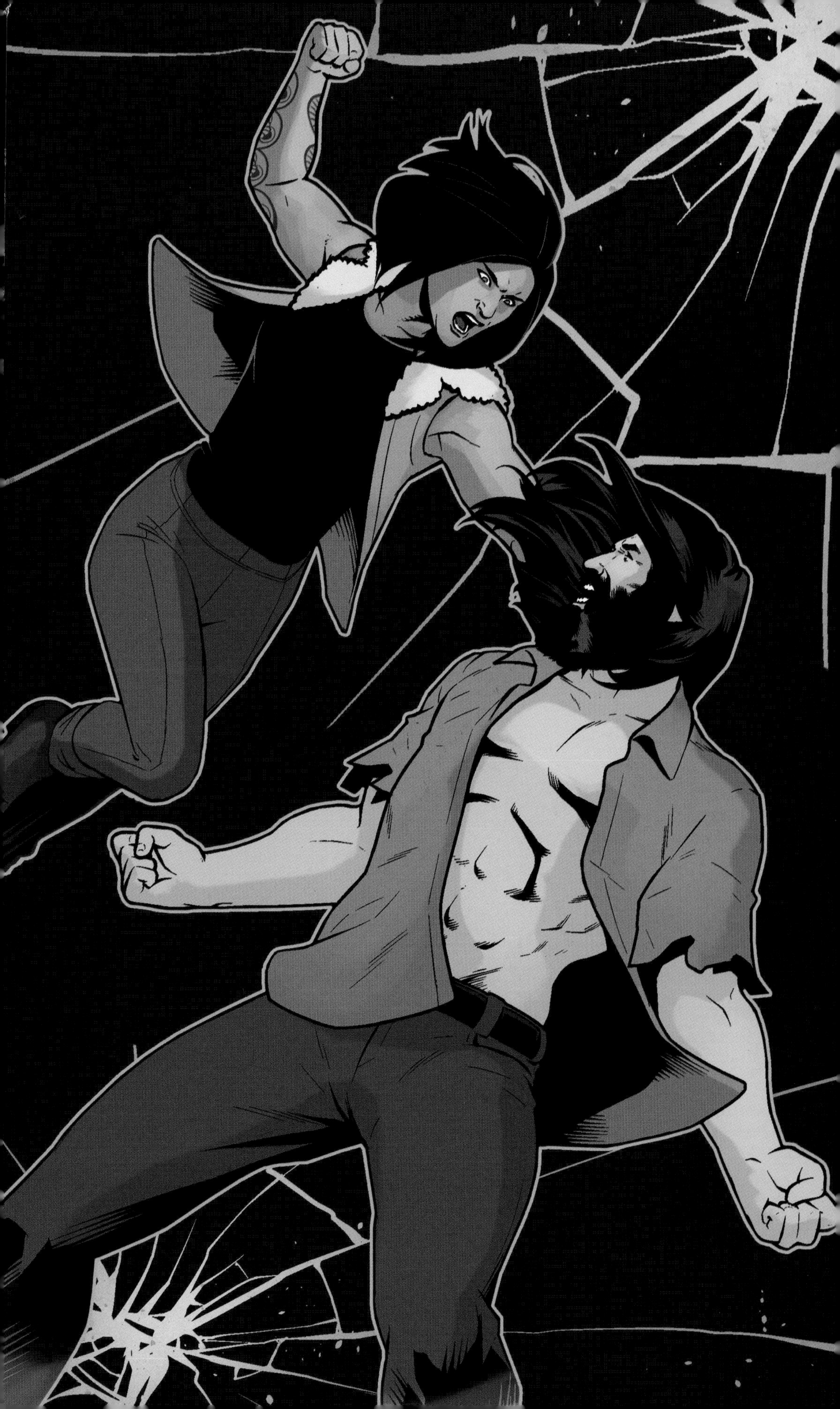

Mama's Boy

By Melanie Scrofano

It's late in the day. Black Badge Division is winding down. Dolls checks his watch. Waverly and Jeremy work together at the computer while, leaning on Dolls' desk, Wynonna absent-mindedly twirls Peacemaker. "Unless you've got something for me to kill, I'm useless here. Think I'll head out." Dolls nods without looking up.

"You got something going on tonight, Dolls?"

"There's a Coyotes game on."

"I know. You want to come by and watch? I've got whiskey with your name on it."

"I don't drink."

"Then just come by and have some wings."

"I don't—"

"Eat? Yeah. You're fun like that. Then just come by and let your body be a temple while I destroy mine and we watch the game. BBD bonding time."

"No."

Wynonna shoots a look at Waverly. Harsh. Dolls catches this.

"I just—I have some paperwork to do." Dolls shrugs. He picks up his jacket and heads out the door. Wynonna turns to Waverly.

"What does that man do when he leaves here? I know he's not hitting up Purgatory's Night Club/Community Center/Kennel Club."

"Ed's Ice Cream Parlor/Pharmacy/Pet Food Shoppe has 2-for-1 protein powder on sale right now," suggests Waverly.

"Maybe it's a woman?" offers Nicole.

Wynonna shoots her a look.

"You're all wrong." Jeremy says confidently. "There's no way he's built like that without maintenance. Based on the caloric needs of a man of 6'1" and 230 lbs. of muscle, he would have to maintain a regimen of eating every two hours along with a crazy training schedule of weights and cardio, minimum 4 days a week."

The team stares at Jeremy, who reddens.

"I may have given this some thought. You know. For science. Waverly, can we get back to work? The Department of Defense isn't going to hack itself."

Wynonna heads for the door, and grabs her leather jacket. Waverly calls out.

"Hey! Where are you going?"

"Research. Don't wait up."

And with that, Wynonna is on her own mission.

Wynonna's Harley slows along the rugged dirt road suffocated by thick woods. The setting sun is mostly blocked out by the trees. It is silent but for the rustle of leaves swaying in the wind and the sound of her engine. If not for Dolls' tire tracks, she would have no idea there was a house in here. She follows the tracks to an opening in the trees, as though someone had cleared a passage just wide enough for a car. The path winds through the trees to a small clearing where she finds a decrepit two-story stone house. It looks abandoned. The smoke coming out of the fireplace suggests otherwise.

This can't be where he really lives. Dolls is not into antiquing. So what is he doing here? If he's cutting up bodies, I'm gonna be pretty disappointed, Wynonna thinks.

Wynonna gets off her bike and walks up the creaking wooden steps of the porch to the front door. She tries it. Locked. She heads to the back of the house, clocking a wood-powered generator and sees the back door is slightly ajar. As quietly as she can, she inches open the door revealing a dark kitchen. The only illumination comes from the last of the daylight through the windows and a few candles. The newness of the gleaming pots and pans, knives, dishes, and linens are a stark contrast to the decaying cupboards and walls. The smell of meat wafts from the wood-fired oven. So he DOES eat... The next room is musty and empty, except for an old couch with ripped upholstery and springs sticking out. Behind it is a door with light coming through the cracks. That's what the generator's for. She opens the door to a flight of stairs set between stone walls. She goes down to the bottom and finds a much heavier looking closed door. She begins to open it, when—

"Wynonna!" She spins around to find Dolls dimly, eerily lit at the top of the stairs. "How did you—?"

"I tracked you. See? I listen. First rule of tracking: 'something something will always something with persistence'." Wynonna's try for levity falls flat. Dolls just stares, immobile.

"So... Are you flipping houses or something?"

His eyes soften, almost childlike. He comes down the stairs.

"Why did you come here?" he asks her.

"I just... Dolls, don't you think it's weird that after all this time, I don't know anything about you? We're a team. I want to know who I'm working with. Who I'm friends with."

In a sudden rage, Dolls grabs Wynonna by the shoulders, pulling her close. "Friends?"

He speaks in a low voice, nearly a whisper.

"We are not friends. I'm your boss and I am not here for you to 'get to know'. I'm here to do a job. That's it. You are just part of the job."

Wynonna's heart sinks. After everything they've been through, watching each other's backs, joking through the danger, was it all just part of the job? How can everything we've been through together mean nothing to you? A fury born from hurt feelings erupts. A stammer forms on her lips, some kind of rebuttal, but she's got nothing and it ends in a frustrated silence.

"Wynonna, for once in your damned life, do yourself a favor and listen to me. Get out of here. Now."

Wynonna glares at him. Defiant to the end, she stands firm.

"No."

He grabs her and roughly spins her, putting himself between her and the mystery door.

"Get out of my house."

"This isn't your house. Your house is an apartment in Purgatory. I followed you there. I saw you get your mail and pretend to go in. I watched you leave out the back and drive the long way here taking detours to cover your tracks."

Dolls tries to keep his cards close to his chest, but a fleeting furrow of his brow betrays his shock.

"I don't know what this place is, but it ain't your house. So I ain't leaving."

He gets in her face, a flash of yellow dashes across his eyes. "You're supposed to be all instinct. What is your instinct telling you right now, Deputy Earp?"

That this is a murder house. Hopefully just a meth lab? But probably a murder house.

"That I should get out of here. But your shady behavior is convincing me that I really want to see what's behind door number one."

Dolls' shoulders fall. "That's the problem with you, Earp. The more I try to scare you, the more you'll want to stay."

Wynonna sees the change in him. "You're my stick-up-your-butt-buddy-in-bad-times. Dolls, whatever is going on here, it can't be that bad."

Dolls looks at her with an expression that lets her know she's about to be proven wrong. From the other side of the door comes a woman's voice, startling Wynonna.

"Baby, lighten your load. Let her in."

Dolls' shoulders slump. He moves out of her way, leaning against the wall, defeated.

"It's over. Fine." Dolls shifts to let Wynonna pass.

Wynonna enters the basement and is surprised that this is the only area of the house with working lights. She searches for the source of the voice. In the far corner of the cellar sits a woman around 60, heavier set, with black hair and grey streaks jetting through it, pulled off her round face in a bun. With the help of her cane, she pushes herself out of her rocking chair and approaches. She walks like someone who doesn't move around much. She looks like Dolls. Her room is pristine. A perfectly made bed, fresh flowers on her nightstand. Behind her is a wall of bookshelves crammed to capacity with books. In front of it, a glider for a reading chair with a table lamp. And surrounding it all, metal prison bars. There is no door in the bars, only one small opening at the bottom wide enough to pass food through.

"Huuuuuuunnhh. Huh?"

The woman laughs. "Dolls did mention that communication skills are not your strong suit." She looks to Dolls.

"Dinner smells good. It isn't turkey meatloaf again, is it? Don't try to trick me, honey. No point in putting me on a diet if I'm staying in here the rest of my life." She looks at Wynonna, driving home the point.

Dolls is quiet. He moves to sit in a chair a few feet away from the bars. He closes his eyes and rests his forehead in his palm, suddenly exhausted looking.

"It's nice to see a fresh face in here, honey. Come here, let me see what the famous Wynonna looks like up close."

Wynonna hesitates, but takes a couple of tentative steps, her curiosity about this woman too much to maintain her distance. "Your face is less symmetrical than I pictured. But still pretty.

"I'm Clarence, Xavier's mama. You must be wondering why Xavier's got me locked up like this?"

"Actually I was. Most people I know keep their moms in the attic, so..." Clarence laughs.

"Oh, that would be nice. A little sunroof, maybe? Not big enough to get out of mind you, but a bit of vitamin D. It's good for the bones. Got me the osteoporosis a few years back. Broke my leg getting out of my chair. Wouldn't have been so bad if we could see a doctor but, well... Dolls did a good job making me a splint. They taught him that in the Army." Clarence looks at him with a mother's pride before laying some mother's guilt. "I try to keep healthy as I can though, because he won't get me help."

"Can't." Dolls speaks up, looking at his mama with a mix of sorrow and frustration. "Not won't. Can't."

"Can't. I know, baby. That's what I meant."

Clarence looks at Wynonna.

"Don't be cross with him for not telling you. He's a good boy just tryin' to do right by his mama and by his moral code and what-not."

"Mama, I don't think this is a good idea."

"Sure it is, honey. It's time to tell her who you really are. Relieve the burden."

Dolls looks to her, to Wynonna, and shakes his head.

"I can tell her if you want, it's been a while since I been able to talk to someone."

Dolls shrugs, looks down to the ground.

Mama leans on her cane, one hand on the bars. Fixes her gaze on Wynonna.

"There was a time, back when Dolls was a boy, I was not... in possession of my truest self. I was..."

"A demon."

Don't say demon. Xavier, you know I don't like when you say demon." Mama turns to Wynonna.

"I was an addict... and a puppet for forces greater than myself. The drug I hungered for was flesh—human and supernatural. The more I had, the stronger I got. The stronger I got, the hungrier I got, and so on until I didn't recognize myself anymore. I was dangerous. BBD was hunting me, so Xavier tried to hide out with me. And one dark night, the darkest of nights, I went into real awful withdrawal. A hunger so deep that even my bones felt empty. And, my own baby... I—"

Clarence is lost in the memory, regret and shame written in the lines of her face.

"...I tried to hurt my own baby Xavier." Clarence looks down. Dolls looks pained for her, for himself.

"It wasn't your fault, mama. I'm okay. Like you said. You weren't yourself."

Clarence's eyes well, she looks at Dolls. "My boy. My good boy."

"So, you're here to protect Dolls?" Wynonna tries to understand.

Dolls gets up and goes to Wynonna. "If it was just about me, I'd never do this to her! I do this to protect her. I do this to protect you and everyone else who can get hurt. If I let her go, she'll kill people, she'll get stronger again, and BBD will eliminate her. They will eliminate my mother. What else am I supposed to do?"

Dolls is very close to Wynonna now.

"What else can I do?" He looks at her in a way that makes Wynonna feel like she should have left when she had the chance.

Clarence addresses Wynonna.

"Wynonna, you've given a lonely old woman and a weary young man a chance to be heard. Thank you for that. Keeping secrets is its own kind of curse, you know."

Dolls leads Wynonna back to the stairwell, his eyes different than Wynonna's ever seen them. They seem freer somehow, with something approaching gratitude and love in his eyes.

"I'm glad you came. I'm sorry I had to keep you in the dark." He stands taller, relieved of the load he was carrying and suddenly aware of how heavy the burden really was.

"It does feel better to let you in, and the secret out...".

Dolls' hands find their way to Wynonna's head, burying themselves in the thick waves of her hair. He kisses her softly; her eyes stay open. Two hearts beating faster, harder.

Then with one deft motion, he snaps her neck.

"...Even if it's just for a moment."

Wynonna falls to the floor, dead.

Dolls' eyes shoot open. He lies there for a minute to catch his breath. He looks at the clock: 5:41 a.m. Then he gets up and gets ready for another day.

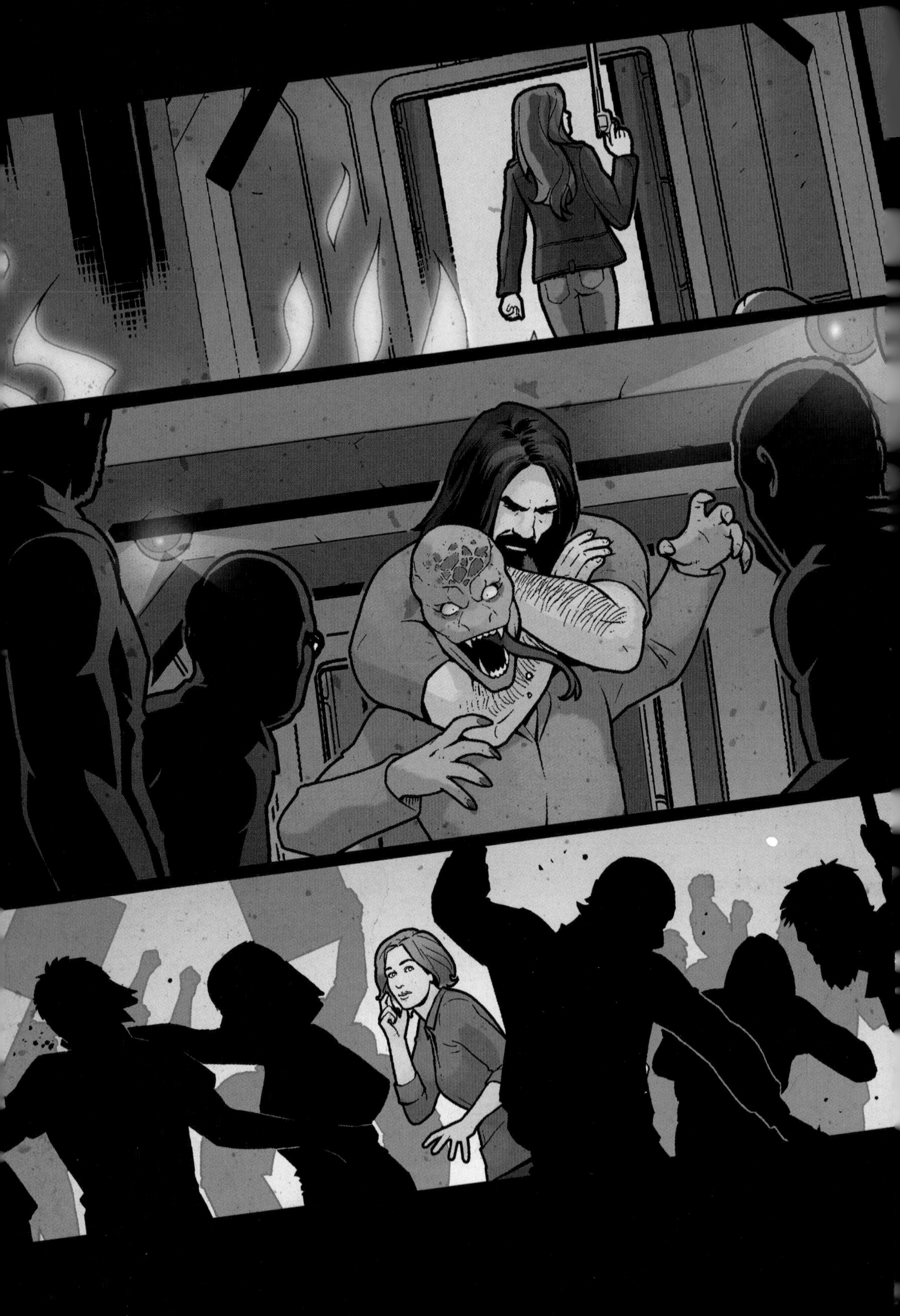